David Paul

New Finding Out 1

Teacher's Book

Macmillan Education
Between Towns Road, Oxford OX4 3PP
A division of Macmillan Publishers Limited
Companies and representatives throughout the world

ISBN-13: 978-1-4050-8083-5
ISBN-10: 1-4050-8083-3

MACMILLAN LANGUAGEHOUSE LTD., Tokyo
ISBN-13: 978-4-7773-6088-8
ISBN-10: 4-7773-6088-1

Design by Anthony Godber
Page make-up by xen
Illustrated by Hiliary Evans
Cover design by Anthony Godber
Cover illustration by Jonatronix

Printed and bound in Thailand

2010   2009   2008   2007   2006
10 9   8   7   6   5   4   3   2   1

Contents

Scope and sequence

Unit	Multi-skill targets *(Listening / Speaking / Reading / Writing)*	Oral targets *(Listening / Speaking)*
1	*Aa, Ee, Ii, Oo, Uu* *What is it? It's a(n) _____ .*	*Hello. What's your name? I'm _____ .*
2	*Bb, Cc, Tt, Dd, Gg*	Numbers 1–12 *What is it? It's a(n) _____ .*
3	*Pp, Nn, Mm, Ss*	*How old are you? I'm _____ .* Things in the room *Touch a _____ .*
4	*Kk, Hh, Qq, Jj*	*How are you? (Fine.)* Days of the week
5	*Ll, Ww, Vv, Ff*	*Goodbye / See you* *I have _____ .* My things
6	*Yy, Zz, Rr, Xx*	Numbers 1–30 Plurals
7	Blending vowels and consonants	*(Very) hot / cold* *What's (cold)?*
8	Three-letter words	
9	Long words	*How do you spell _____ ?*
10	*What is it? It's a(n) _____ .*	*I don't know.* *I like _____s.*
11	*ee, ea, ch, sh* (words / sentences)	
12	*oo, o͞o, ar, ou* (words / sentences)	
13	*Is it a _____ ?* *Yes, it is. / No, it isn't.*	Months of the year *My birthday is in _____ .*
14	*o͞r, ir, ow, oy* (words / sentences)	
15	*oa, o͞w, ay, ai* (words / sentences)	

Introduction

1 The Questioning Approach

(The theory behind New Finding Out)

The *Questioning Approach* is a general humanistic approach to learning English that has been developed in Hiroshima, Japan. The following chapter outlines the approach as it relates to *New Finding Out* Level 1. All examples are appropriate for elementary school children who are learning English for the first time.

How a child learns

Children are active learners and have a natural tendency to be inquisitive. From an early age, they try to make sense of the world around them by exploring and asking questions. When their explorations are successful, their confidence increases and they are encouraged to ask more and more questions. However, if they experience too many failures or the answers to their questions do not fit together to form clear patterns, they are likely to lose motivation and either turn their attention in other directions or become less interested in exploring.

In the *Questioning Approach* to learning English, this natural inquisitiveness is nurtured and strengthened, particularly by leading the children toward a succession of language targets that are achievable and can easily be related to each other. The more the children succeed and the more that English makes sense to them, the less afraid they will be of making mistakes. Increasingly, they will be able to face uncontrolled language with confidence and a sense of adventure.

However, each time that a child successfully discovers a language target, she must feel that it is a result of her own exploration; it is not just some information she is receiving from the teacher. Learning is a deeply personal experience. For a child to learn new language successfully, to the extent that she can remember and produce it spontaneously, she needs to personally experience each stage of the following Questioning Cycle.

The Questioning Cycle

Many discipline and motivation problems in class result from a failure to regularly complete this Questioning Cycle. In fact, the process of building a child's confidence and encouraging a positive attitude toward English is very delicate, and neglecting any of the stages of the Questioning Cycle may have serious long-term consequences.

Stage 1: She notices something new
In *New Finding Out*, her attention is drawn to a new English word or pattern presented in a puzzle that is fun and attractive. It could be a card in a game, a mime, a word in a song, natural interaction in a dialogue, and so on.

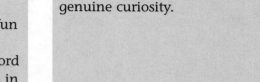

Stage 2: She wonders what it is
She is given space to wonder, feel curious and make guesses so as to generate and stimulate genuine curiosity.

Stage 3: She tries to find out what it is
In *New Finding Out*, she generally learns English questions to express her curiosity and then uses these questions to discover new words and patterns. On other occasions, she tries to guess the meaning of an English question. In either case, the objective is to build up her motivation and give her the tools to explore the world of English with a sense of adventure.

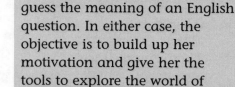

A sense of adventure

Each time the Questioning Cycle is successfully completed, the child will feel it is safer to risk being curious. Her natural sense of adventure will be strengthened. She will ask more and more questions, and so she will learn.

One of the main adversaries of this sense of adventure is dependency. A child needs love and encouragement, and she needs to feel that the teacher is on her side, but she needs as little direct help as possible. This does not mean the teacher should say "Do it yourself!" in an unloving way or complain that a child should be more independent. Children are what they are; some are more independent than others, and that is hardly their fault. However, learning, rather than "being taught," is an adventure that is best undertaken with a certain amount of independence. When a child grows older and has chances to speak or write English, there will be no teacher to help her.

The objective is for each child to explore and practice language as much as possible by herself. She should feel that it is her game, not the teacher's; it is her puzzle that she wants to solve by herself. The teacher gives hints when the child experiences difficulty but does not provide the whole answer unless there is no alternative. For example, the teacher may say one word to prompt the child to make a whole sentence, or underline a part of a word that has been misspelled rather than immediately telling her the correct spelling. The child should be given a chance to "find out" correct answers for herself. The teacher helps and gives enough warm encouragement to give the child confidence to try for herself, and then withdraws.

If a child's sense of adventure is not encouraged, she tends to draw a defensive barrier around the familiar world and make a clear distinction between what she knows and what she does not know. One of the reasons that methods such as repetition after the teacher and memorization weaken a child's sense of adventure is that they reinforce this distinction between the known and the unknown. For example, if a child memorizes the reading of words, she tends to distinguish between the words she knows and the words she has not yet memorized. In *New Finding Out*, every new word she learns is seen as a gateway to many more words. (See also *An active approach to phonics*, page 28.)

Trial and error

When a child simply receives knowledge from a teacher, very little exploration or experimentation is involved, and little real learning takes place. To really learn English so that she can use it with

---

Stage 4: She finds out
In the early stages of learning, she must "find out." She will make many mistakes while she is experimenting with new language, and this is very healthy, but she must be able to learn new language before she loses interest in it. It is important to avoid confusing or frustrating her by arousing her interest in language that is too difficult for her to learn.

Stage 5: She plays with the language
She practices and practices, trying out new words and patterns and learning from her mistakes. When she does make mistakes, the teacher gives hints and encourages her to "find out" what her mistakes are. When practicing, she does not repeat language mechanically. Instead, she plays games where she can repeat the language many times and still feel emotionally involved with it.

Stage 6: She relates the language to her previous experience
As she practices, she links the new language with the English she already knows. She senses patterns and uses these patterns to help her make guesses about the next new language she encounters. She needs to feel that the English she learns fits together and is not just a mass of loosely related language points. This can best be achieved through games where she is challenged to practice and connect both new and old language targets.

feeling and spontaneity, a child needs to play with it, test theories and learn from her mistakes. She should practice and practice and discover patterns for herself.

The child also needs emotional support and encouragement from the teacher, and she needs to be protected from encountering language that is beyond her ability and may weaken her desire to explore. However, she does not need direct help from the teacher while there is still a chance that she can make a discovery for herself.

In *New Finding Out*, when new language is presented, the child is encouraged to make guesses and anticipate what the language might be before discovering it. After making the discovery, she practices the language in games and learns by using it and making mistakes. The same principle applies when writing; she writes and writes, gradually learning by trial and error.

Communicative context

In the *Questioning Approach*, language is always learned in context. Grammar is never treated as an academic exercise and words are never learned in isolation. Notice the difference between the following three methods of introducing vocabulary:

1 Isolated words
The teacher holds up a picture of an apple and the class repeats *apple, apple* … . It is a little surprising how widely this method is used.

2 In a sentence
The teacher holds up the picture and the class repeats *It's an apple. It's an apple* … . This is definitely an improvement on the previous method, but it is still rather artificial and teacher-centered.

3 Questioning (used in *New Finding Out*)
The teacher half-draws a picture, mimes an animal very quickly, hides a picture, etc. She teases the children a little, perhaps by drawing just a little more of a picture or miming an animal even more quickly. She stimulates their curiosity until they really want to know what the picture is in English. She has not generated the feeling *It's an ant* but the feeling *What is it?*, so it is the question that she feeds.

The teacher encourages the children to say *What is it? What is it?* with slightly dramatic intonation. When they really want to know, they discover the answer *It's an ant* with the teacher. (See *Advice and techniques*, page 16, for further discussion of this technique.)

In the above example, a picture of an ant rather than of a more familiar animal or object is used because it is unlikely that the children will already know what it is in English, so they are more likely to genuinely have the feeling *What is it?* Once the question and answer have been practiced a few times, it is no longer necessary to elicit this specific feeling of curiosity. Instead, spontaneous use of the question-answer pattern is maintained by practicing it in games.

A child's view of English

In the *Questioning Approach*, the objective is for each child to feel that she is discovering English for herself. Even though the teacher is, in fact, leading her in a specific direction, each child should feel that she is learning what she genuinely wants to learn. New targets are presented as puzzles for her to solve, and her interest in solving these puzzles helps her feel that learning English is personal and "real," not just a classroom exercise.

The deeper and more genuine a child's curiosity in a new language, the more likely it is that she will deeply internalize it and be able to produce it spontaneously. She should sense patterns, not simply understand them as rational rules, and these patterns should certainly never be analyzed by the teacher. Real learning is an emotional, not a rational, experience.

Each child will develop her own ideas about how English works and use these ideas to make predictions about new language she meets. The clearer her ideas, the more positive she will be about making predictions. Conversely, the more confused and misty the relationship between the language targets she has learned, the less confidence she will have to explore new language and the more likely it is that she will just wait to be "taught." The sequence of language in *New Finding Out* has been designed so that new targets can be comfortably linked to previous targets to form clear patterns.

A child's ideas about English become even clearer if new language is approached from a number of different directions. For example, only being able to speak language tends to leave it hanging in midair, but being able to read and write it as well makes it much more secure – one skill links with another skill. In *New Finding Out*, all the main target language is spoken, read, written, played with in a variety of games, mixed with previously learned language and continually reviewed.

The reality of a child

Learning English should be as "real" an experience as possible for a child. An unsuccessful lesson feels like a classroom exercise and appears to originate in the world of the teacher, not the child. In a successful lesson, the child's world is gradually widened. It is essential for the teacher to understand this world and for the child to feel that the lesson begins in it. What does feel real to a child in the classroom?

Her emotions feel real

We should try to generate an emotional interest in language before it is learned, and this emotional involvement should continue as the language is practiced. For example, amusing pictures of animals generate more emotion than pictures of tables and pencils, absurdities are often more fun than dry examples, games are more enjoyable than drills and slightly dramatic intonation has more impact than straight intonation. Lessons should be fun and contain as much humor as possible.

Her daily life feels real

Wherever possible, language should be personalized. Questions like *How old are you?* or *Where is your school?* are more real than *How old is John?* or *Where is the school?* A child's family, friends, city and interests are all real to her.

The classroom feels real

It is always preferable to relate language to objects or pictures that a child can see and feel. She should touch and play with the flashcards or toys that we bring into the class, use objects that are in the classroom or in her bag as examples, and interact with the other children in the class as much as possible.

Games feel real

We only have to see the relief on a child's face when she is released from an academic class and can run and play with her friends to see that games are at the core of her sense of reality. The more we can make learning into a game, the more real it will feel to her.

The English she already knows feels real

She should encounter language that can easily be related to and built onto what she already knows. *New Finding Out* has been written with this principle very much in mind.

What she wants to say feels real

For example, before a child learns *What is it?*, the teacher should set up a situation so that she genuinely wants to say *What is it?* Also, if she says something like *It's hot!* spontaneously in her own language and if the English equivalent is achievable, we can feed the translation.

"Learning" vs. "being taught"

If the teacher begins a lesson with explanation, demonstration, repetition after the teacher or any other method that originates in the teacher's world, the children immediately fall into the role of those who are being "taught." Effective learning begins in the reality of the child.

The more children receive from a teacher, the fewer questions they need to ask, the fewer adventures into the unknown they need to take and the more they wait to be taught. In the short term, children can get knowledge from being "taught," but the long-term effect on their desire to learn can be disastrous. We can go so far as to say that the more teachers "teach," the less children "learn."

Real learning takes place when the child is asking questions that originate in her reality, when she feels that she is "finding out" the answers to these questions herself and when she is able to link these answers with others she has already discovered to form patterns that make sense to her. It is the assumption of the *Questioning Approach* that the regular successful completion of this Questioning Cycle is at the root of all real learning.

A comparison with some other approaches

The *Questioning Approach* is an approach to learning English in which a clear language syllabus, arranged in incremental and achievable steps, is "learned" in fun activities, not "taught" by the teacher. In this chapter, the *Questioning Approach* is contrasted with some alternative ways of teaching English to children. For the sake of clarity, approaches are divided into categories – though, of course, many approaches fall into more than one of the categories considered.

Teacher-centered approaches

At the core of any teacher-centered approach is the belief that teachers teach and so children learn – the initiative comes from the teacher. The effect of this belief can be seen not only in the traditional classroom, but also in methods such as repetition after the teacher or mechanical drilling, and even in individual teachers using the most progressive approaches.

In the *Questioning Approach*, the word "teach" is never used. Teachers do not "teach"; children "learn." Lessons are planned by the teacher and the children are led toward pre-determined targets, so in a sense the teacher does have the initiative. However, the crucial factor is how the children feel about this. There are approaches, particularly some versions of the situational and communicative approaches, that on a rational level are very student-centered but that on an emotional level do not feel so to the children. In the *Questioning Approach*, rationally much initiative remains in the hands of the teacher, but the objective is for each child to feel that she is learning for herself.

Structural approaches

There are a number of approaches that emphasize the necessity of learning a clear sequence of grammatical structures. In some, grammatical rules are analyzed and explained either in English or in the learner's language, while in others these rules are learned by induction. The *Questioning Approach* places emphasis on the learning of grammar by induction in the early stages of learning, so *New Finding Out*, being designed for young children, may

at first sight appear a fairly traditional, structured course.

One of the main differences from most structural approaches is the emphasis on creating an emotional need for language before it is discovered. Another is that, in the *Questioning Approach*, the learning of structures is not valued for its own sake. Instead it is seen as a way of helping children discover connections between the individual items of language they are learning. When the children sense a pattern, they may use it to make guesses about new items of language they encounter. So grammar, like phonics, provided it is "learned" rather than "taught," can strengthen a child's ability and confidence to learn with a sense of adventure.

A third difference is the degree to which new language is linked with previously learned language. In many structural approaches, it is considered a virtue to teach clear and independent targets in each lesson and then to have review sections of a lesson or whole review lessons for bringing all the targets together. In the *Questioning Approach*, the objective is for old and new language to be constantly linked and practiced together. In *New Finding Out*, this has mainly been achieved through the games, which have been designed to achieve maximum linking, and the exercises in the Home Book, particularly the crosswords, where new and old language are mixed together.

Natural approaches

There is a widespread belief that the English as a foreign language classroom should approximate the conditions under which children learn their native language. Many of the methods resulting from this belief remind teachers of how they learned their own language when they were children, and so have a natural appeal.

The key difference between the *Questioning Approach* and natural approaches concerns the use of time. Many children who are learning English as a foreign language, rather than as their native language or as a second language, have very little time to learn – often only one or two hours a week. Under these circumstances, if they learn "naturally," they generally make very little progress. In the *Questioning Approach*, emphasis is placed on the efficient use of time.

Let us look at some of the main principles that natural approaches have in common and see how the *Questioning Approach* differs.

1 Children should discover English for themselves

One principle that is shared by most natural approaches is that children should be allowed to explore and discover English for themselves. This is also a core principle of the *Questioning Approach*. The difference is the extent to which the children are encouraged to explore in a specific direction. The objective is for the children to feel that they are discovering language for themselves, but for the teacher to have a very clear idea of where the course is going. It is the children's feeling that is crucial. As long as the learning process feels real to them, there is no contradiction, and time is used more efficiently.

2 The input of language is crucial

Another principle is that being exposed to English of an appropriate level is more important than being trained to produce language. However, most of the convincing case studies either concern children learning their native language or a foreign language in a country where the language is spoken all around them.

There is little evidence to suggest that children learning English as a foreign language in their own country and studying for only a short time each week will benefit very much from just being exposed to comprehensible language. There is definitely a need for children to simply enjoy listening to English – with *New Finding Out*, My CD (found in the Class Book) is aimed at satisfying this need. It is also essential for children to be encouraged to read by themselves as much as possible. However, in the classroom, children seem to respond much more positively and gain much more from learning and using productive skills. Also, in cultures where children are encouraged to be dependent and passive learners, it is particularly important to establish an independent and active learning pattern in the early stages. *New Finding Out* has been written in Japan, where dependency is often a serious problem and attempts by teachers to use methods that emphasize the input rather than the output of language often serve to encourage a passive attitude, which the children find it difficult to ever break out of.

3 Children learn best by playing games and singing songs

A third idea, which derives from the way children learn their native language, is that children learn best by playing games, singing songs and generally experiencing English with their senses. Controlling the language in these activities is often not considered particularly important.

In the *Questioning Approach*, too, playing games and learning with the senses play the central role in lessons, but controlling the language content of games and songs is considered vital. With native speakers or children learning English as a second language, there is much to be said for using less controlled language, but the needs of foreign language learners are different. If the language in games and songs is directly related to the targets of the course, not only is more efficient use made of the limited time available and the children given a clearer direction, but they are also not exposed to too much language, which may be confusing and weaken their positivity and motivation.

When the language content is not a main priority and activities are chosen more for their popularity than for the language being practiced, there are many dangers. It is often the case that games and songs that are popular are repeated over and over again, long after children have internalized the language for which they were designed. This may lead to the language being reproduced rather mechanically and the course losing momentum.

Games and songs that are played for their own sake tend to be used as rewards or as a way of maintaining discipline. For many children, the learning of English comes to be regarded as "studying" and the playing of games as "fun." Learning itself can be fun, especially if it is successful. Children are naturally curious about the world around them and enjoy exploring it. They enjoy asking questions. In the *Questioning Approach*, the teacher encourages this inquisitiveness, gives the children the language tools to express their curiosity and makes sure they "find out" the answers with minimum frustration.

Discovering language is like playing with a new toy. Enjoyable games and songs are an essential and integral part of this process, but they are always used to reinforce the language in the course. There is never any differentiation between the "studying" part of a lesson and the "fun" part; it is all fun.

Other humanistic approaches

In a sense, all approaches to teaching are humanistic or at least contain humanistic elements. However, the approaches that are generally referred to as humanistic are those that place particular emphasis on the personal nature of learning and see the teacher's role as secondary and supportive.

One of the main problems faced by many approaches of this kind is that they are out of reach of the inexperienced teacher. With the *Questioning Approach*, this is not a problem, as the key techniques are easy to learn and use.

Proponents of humanistic approaches often feel that more traditional courses are too rigid and insensitive to the deeper learning needs of students. Those teachers who favor traditional approaches often feel that humanistic approaches make inefficient use of time and fail to give the students a clear sense of direction. The *Questioning Approach* attempts to reconcile these two viewpoints.

In the *Questioning Approach*, courses and individual lessons are carefully planned in advance, the targets are pre-determined, maximum use is made of the time available and the students are given a very clear sense of direction. However, learning is regarded as something very personal and emotional, new language is introduced in a way that feels "real" to the students, and the teacher's role is supportive and peripheral. The students are able to learn all the language structures that have traditionally been considered important, but they are able to retain a much higher percentage of the language they encounter and produce it more spontaneously because the teacher employs a humanistic approach.

2 The components of *New Finding Out*

1 The Class Book

The Class Book defines the language to be learned in the course. It is bright and colorful in order to attract the interest of the children in class and so that they will enjoy looking at it by themselves or with their parents at home. There are fifteen units in the book. Each unit represents a stage of learning, not a fixed number of lessons.

Multi-skill targets

These are the words and patterns in each unit that can be spoken, read and written, and integrated with the multi-skill targets learned in previous units. It is the children's success in internalizing these targets that determines how much real progress they are making.

If the children can just hear and say these targets, it will be necessary to review the targets many times. If they can read as well, they will be able to make more real progress. And if they can write these targets in dictation exercises or in personalized sentences, the children are most likely to be reaching their full potential as learners. It is the balance of skills, with one skill supporting and deepening the others, that leads to the greatest internalization of new words and patterns.

Oral-only targets

The oral-only targets in each unit serve a number of important purposes. They are an effective way to provide early practice of a word or pattern that will later become a core multi-skill target. This makes it easier for children to internalize them more deeply later on. They give the children a chance to practice conversation patterns that they cannot read or write yet, but that they can immediately use in practical situations. They also give the children a chance to encounter important words that may be difficult to read and write at that stage of learning.

Activities

Phonics

The Phonics pages introduce the basic sounds and letters of English. These are the core of *New Finding Out 1*, and children learn to recognize them in listening and reading activities, and use them in speaking and writing activities.

Conversation

These activities introduce useful daily conversation patterns for children to say.

Phonic words

These words use sounds the children are learning. Until Unit 10, children practice the words orally; after that they can also read and write them.

Games

These games can be used for learning, practicing and combining together a wide variety of language targets in an enjoyable and motivating context.

Listen / Read and draw

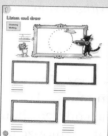

These activities encourage children to use the phonics skills they are learning to discover both familiar and new words and record them in a creative way.

Action song

The action songs in *New Finding Out* create a multi-sensory environment where children practice and learn words and patterns. The melody, rhythm and actions all combine to create a positive learning context.

Exercise

These activities give children more practice in reading and writing the target language.

Dictation

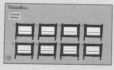

These activities give children practice in listening to and writing the target language.

Words in action

These pages contain two communicative activities that encourage children to use and personalize new words and patterns.

Word set

These pages present useful vocabulary orally. Many of these words are difficult to read and write at this stage.

Combining sounds

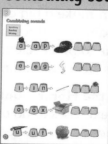

These activities show children how the phonics sounds they have learnt can be blended together.

Phonic families

These games encourage children to identify patterns based on phonic sounds, and to use these to explore new words.

Target pattern

These pages introduce simple, high-frequency structures for children to say, read and write.

Building fluency

These activities build the children's ability to quickly switch from one pattern to another in longer and longer dialogues.

2 The Home Book

The Home Book is intended for use at home between lessons. It is divided into units in the same way as the Class Book. A typical unit looks like this:

The objective of the Home Book

Being able to practice the target language at home between lessons can make a big difference to how much of it they retain. In particular, it is often difficult to find time to practice enough writing in class, so this skill is emphasized in the Home Book.

How soon to use the Home Book

It is best to assign exercises to do at home from the very first lesson and establish a regular pattern of using the Home Book between lessons. The pace of the Home Book is dictated by the pace of the Class Book: the children should never be further along in the Home Book than they are in the Class Book.

Keeping up

Ideally, the children should all do the exercises in the Home Book at a similar pace. Serious level difference problems may develop in class if some children do not keep up in the Home Book.

Showing the children what to do

Before being asked to do any of the exercises in the Home Book, the children need to be shown exactly what they are expected to do. Whenever possible, a similar exercise should be done in class. If a child fails to keep up in the Home Book, it may be that she is not clear about what to do.

Correcting

It is always a good idea to look at any of the work the children have done in the Home Book. One way of doing this is to set aside a section of the lesson for checking and going through the homework. If the class is not too large, the children can correct the homework with the teacher. Another way is for the teacher to correct the homework with each individual child in turn; this can be done during a writing activity so that all the other children have something to do. (See *Hinting and withdrawing*, page 16, for more ideas on correction.)

3 My CD

My CD is included with each Class Book. The objective is for the children to listen to the CD regularly at home or in the car. The children should not feel that they have to listen to it, memorize it or that they are going to be tested on it. They should be encouraged to relax and enjoy it.

4 The Class Audio Recording

The Class Audio Recording is for teachers who would like to use a recording in class. It contains the vocabulary, dialogues and songs that are in the Class Book. It also contains versions of the songs without the words. For teachers who are not native speakers of English, the pronunciation on the tape may be particularly helpful, especially when the children are learning phonics.

The recordings are primarily intended for consolidation of new words and patterns, not for introducing them. (See *How to use the Guide*, page 31, for specific recommendations on when to use the recording.) New language is always discovered by the children, not received from the teacher or a recording. There are, of course, some cases where listening to a song or a dialogue on a recording may be a kind of puzzle for the children to solve, but even in these cases we need to be sure the children are thinking and guessing, not just copying or parroting the recording.

5 The Flashcards

There is a set of flashcards to accompany each level of the course. It is not absolutely necessary to use these, but it is strongly recommended. Each card has a picture on one side and text on the other side.

The arrangement of the cards

The cards are divided into categories. For Level 1, the categories are as follows:

1 Alphabet   **2** Vocabulary A
3 Double Letters   **4** Vocabulary B

The cards for each level have the same color symbol as the Class Book and Home Book for that level. The color for Level 1 is yellow.

6 The Teacher's CD-ROM

There is one Teacher's CD-ROM for each level of *New Finding Out*. The CD-ROM includes resources for classroom activities, planning, assessment and teacher development.

Classroom resources

The Teacher's CD-ROM contains **Full-size flashcards** to accompany the Word set pages (and in higher levels, the Forming sentences pages). It also provides **Small flashcards** that can be printed out to provide individual sets for children or groups. These small color flashcards include all the pictures and words from the Flashcard pack, as well as the Word set flashcards.

Equipment for games can also be found on the CD-ROM. This includes all the **Photocopiable masters** from this Teacher's Book (see pages 127–150), which can be printed in color from the CD-ROM, and the **Phonic families racetracks**, which can be enlarged and/or laminated to create class sets.

Course management resources

The Teacher's CD-ROM provides a range of templates to assist with planning and assessment. Each CD-ROM contains a **Planning template**, which details the language covered in each unit and gives space to record what language was reviewed, what activities were used (and which the children particularly enjoyed) and what homework was set. As well as being a useful resource for the class teacher, this can be invaluable for a teacher who finds himself/herself covering a class with which she is unfamiliar.

The Teacher's CD-ROM also contains assessment materials suitable for the level. These consist of several templates for **Assessment activities**, along with teaching notes. The templates can be used to assess the language from a specific unit or a number of units. The activities are designed to be communicative and child-centered, in line with the general approach of *New Finding Out*, but their flexibility allow the teacher to decide whether to re-use or vary activities for assessment at different points in the level.

For the end of the level, the Teacher's CD-ROM contains a color **Certificate**, which can be printed and presented to children on completion of the book. In addition, the Teacher's CD-ROM provides a **Progress report template**, which allows the teacher to quickly complete a report to be printed and given to the child's parents. The report details the child's progress with respect to language targets, as well as indicating behavior and providing the parents with suggestions for ways in which to help their child. All the information is given in English and the child's home language.

Teacher development

The Teacher's CD-ROM contains a list of useful **Web links** and a **Bibliography**, as well as details of how to access and join the **Active Learners** web-based discussion group, where teachers using *Finding Out* have been sharing ideas, materials, questions and advice since 2004. David Paul moderates and contributes frequently to the group, which has more than a hundred members.

Information on supplementary resources

You will find information on the Teacher's CD-ROM about **Supplementary resources** that complement *New Finding Out*, which are also referenced where appropriate in the teaching notes. The materials include Reading rods, Phonics builders and additional worksheets available on CD-ROM, and many of them have been produced by teachers using *Finding Out*.

These resources are not produced by Macmillan, and Macmillan takes no responsibility for their quality or availability.

3 Advice and techniques

The role of the teacher

Being one of the class

The children need to feel that the teacher is one of the class. When we talk to a child, we should try to avoid making her feel that we are teaching, explaining or talking down to her. We want her to feel that we enjoy being with her and care about her. Sitting among the children (rather than in the teacher's chair or standing in an intimidating position) can also help to achieve the right kind of relationship.

The objective is for the children to feel that we are discovering new language with them. It all seems new and fascinating for us, too. They should not feel that we already know all the answers. If we appear too confident, it may both weaken the children's confidence and make them less likely to accept us as an insider in their group.

Some teachers may feel that we lose authority or that the children's confidence in us is undermined if we ever appear ignorant in class, but this is usually not so. If we insist on being right, it is likely that the children will either lose interest because the lesson is the teacher's game and does not originate in their world or they will tend to become passive and wait to receive knowledge. Their confidence in us is more likely to be determined by their success or failure in solving the puzzles that we put in their path, and whether or not they can link and make sense of the language we lead them toward.

Providing a clear direction

It is important that we carefully prepare all lessons in advance and that each lesson has a clear target. At each stage of the lesson we should know what activity to do next, and at the end of the lesson the children should have a clear idea of what they have learned and a sense of accomplishment. The course needs an inner momentum. There should be plenty of review throughout the course, but the children also need to feel that they are moving forward. They should make steady progress, constantly linking new language with what they already know.

When language is presented, there should be no ambiguity about what language is being targeted. For example, when we want the children to learn the question *What is it?*, we should encourage the children to want to ask this question rather than another question like *Where is it?* or *What's it doing?* This Teacher's Book contains many specific suggestions on how to achieve this, and the Flashcards have been designed to elicit unambiguous targets.

Presenting language attractively

The colorful Flashcards and Class Book help to make the language targets attractive. If we appear fascinated by these materials, the children probably will be, too. It is also important to smile and appear very positive whenever new language is introduced. As a teacher gains more experience with the approach used in this book, it becomes apparent that all language targets can be introduced in activities where children are focused and making guesses. There is no need for a teacher to pre-teach. The children may discover new words or patterns inside a game, in an appealing story or in a dialogue where they are having genuine interaction with the teacher or each other.

Hinting and withdrawing

We should talk as little as possible and try not to be the center of attention. The children should feel they are experiencing language directly rather than through the teacher.

If a child cannot produce any language or makes a mistake, we hint and withdraw. The hint may be a gesture, a picture, a word or something like an amusing sound to indicate that there has been a mistake, and it is always the minimum necessary to encourage the child to discover the correct language for herself.

Hints should be given tentatively. If we give them with too much authority, there is a danger that we will slip into the formal "teacher" role and the child into a dependent one. We should encourage her to feel that a game is being played and be careful not to make her feel that she has done something wrong. One very effective way of achieving this is for us to use a puppet or stuffed animal to give hints and motivate her to pause and reflect on and try and figure out what the mistake is.

If she makes a mistake when writing, we can underline the letter or word that is wrong and let her search for the correct answer. If she cannot find it, we can give a little more help, gradually leading her in the right direction.

If necessary, we can "feed" words or patterns the children are searching for. This means that we introduce new language in such a way that each child feels she is discovering it with the teacher, not repeating it after the teacher. For example:

Not: **Teacher**   *Please repeat: "What is it?"*
      Children   *What is it?*

But: **Teacher**   Appears puzzled by a picture or object, begins to mouth the word what and smiles as if to say *How do we say that?* The teacher empathizes with the children's feeling and leads them toward the question *What is it?* by gently saying it in stages. The children join in and should feel they are discovering that question with the teacher.

Getting all the children involved

There is a danger that classes will be dominated by one or two children. The objective is for each child to be learning, not for some children to learn and the others to follow them.

One of the main roles of the teacher is to make sure that each child has an equal chance to speak. With some classes, it may be necessary to adapt activities to encourage quieter children to join in. An example of this would be to adapt a game so that questions are directed at individual children rather than letting them compete with each other (for example, see Unit 1, **Slam game**).

Behavior problems

One of the most difficult questions for proponents of child-centered learning to face up to is what to do with children who have trouble following classroom rules. Answering this question is made more difficult by the realization that most of the children have very little time to learn English, and behavior problems in a class may seriously slow down the pace of learning.

Here are a few ideas that may help:

1 Encourage the feeling that learning English is a game that has rules

We should establish these rules as soon as possible, not by explaining them but by responding to the first transgression of each rule. We can be clear about the rules without being authoritarian or making the children feel that we do not trust or love them.

What we do in the first one or two lessons will generally become the norm for a while. For example, if we want only English to be used during the course, we should ensure that no native language is used from the first lesson. Of course, we should not insist on this in an intimidating way.

2 Be consistent in enforcing these rules

If we decide that there is a rule against running around the classroom, crawling under the table, translating targets into the native language and so on, we should be consistent in our way of dealing with each type of transgression.

3 Try to understand why there is a problem

How we respond to a consistent problem depends on the reason for the problem. It may be because one of the children finds the lessons difficult, in which case we can give her extra help. It may be because she finds the lessons easy, in which case we can try to get her interested in helping some of the other children. Before dealing with a problem it is important to try and understand its cause.

4 Use puppets or stuffed animals

Rules can be enforced and points awarded by a puppet or stuffed animal. We remain smiling, but the puppet or stuffed animal can be stricter. This can make discipline a lot of fun.

5 Give the children attention

If children lose concentration, it can be difficult to keep the lesson going in the desired direction. If we can, we need to give a child attention before her attention slips. We may just need to smile at her, call her name, move near her, make a fun sound, or greet her with a puppet or toy animal.

6 Encourage the children to want to behave well

Points can be awarded to another team when one of the children doesn't play a game in English, crawls under a table and so on. The objective is to encourage other children in the same team to turn to the child who is misbehaving and say *"Speak English!"* or *"Don't do that!"* Instead of points, there could be a game running through the lessons – for example, there could be a soccer scoring system along the top of the board, and when one team behaves badly the ball is moved towards their goal. And, of course, it could be a puppet or stuffed animal that awards the points or moves the ball.

7 Change the seating positions
Problems often arise because children form smaller groups within a class. If this begins to happen, the children's seating positions may need to be changed. It is also a good idea if we vary where we sit in the class. We can sit near any child who is disrupting the class, but we should do this casually without giving her too much special attention.

8 Maintain a stimulating pace
Many problems can be pre-empted by keeping the pace of a lesson fast and stimulating. Maintaining the children's interest in English by making the lesson fun and exciting can prevent most behavior problems from arising.

9 Ensure success
Make sure the language targets and activities are achievable, and make sure the children come away from an activity and the lesson as a whole with a sense of accomplishment. When necessary, we may need to break down the targets and the activities into more manageable stages.

10 Treat the children as real people
Know and use the children's names. In a large class, each child may need a nametag. Join in the games and relax with the children. Tease them in a friendly way and play with them. Have special class events. In fact, do everything possible to create a sense of "community" in the class where each individual child feels valued.

The role of the children

The center of learning
Learning originates in the children's world (see *The Questioning Approach*, page 6). Language is never explained or repeated after the teacher mechanically. It is presented as an intriguing puzzle, which each child discovers how to solve. It is then used in ways that emphasize the position of the child as the center of learning.

Asking questions
If we ask questions like *What is it?*, *Is it a cat?* or *It's a cat, true or false?*, the initiative originates in our world, not the children's. It is the children who should be asking the questions.

In *New Finding Out*, children learn questions before learning answers, and they use these questions as tools to express their curiosity. They learn *What is it?* before *It's a cat,* and they continue to learn and practice new vocabulary by asking and answering questions about it.

Practicing and making mistakes
The objective is for the children to sense patterns and rules in English by using them. They practice and practice, try out theories, make mistakes and practice again. When they make mistakes, we give them hints, they try to correct their mistakes and then they continue practicing.

Most of the oral and reading practice is in the form of games. When the children play games, they use new language again and again, mixing it with language from past units; they make mistakes and learn from these mistakes.

When practicing writing, they write letters, words or question-answer patterns many times, gradually discovering how to write English correctly. (See *Reading and writing*, page 29.)

Pair practice and group work
Some classes respond better to pair work and group work than others. There are many activities in *New Finding Out* that are done in pairs, and these are particularly important for getting the focus of the lesson away from the teacher; but if the children seem to be feeling pressure from these activities, it is best to switch to something else and introduce the idea of pair practice more gradually.

In general, pair work is more effective than working in groups of three or four because each child has more time to speak and the shy children tend to be more directly involved. However, activities where the class is divided into two groups that compete as teams are very effective for increasing motivation and getting all the children involved.

"Teaching" the teacher

Whenever possible, the children can show the teacher how to do a new exercise. The teacher looks at the exercise, appears puzzled by it and appeals to the children for help. The children, as a team, figure out what to do and "teach" the teacher. (For example, see Unit 8, **Crossword**.) This encourages the children not only to feel more valuable, but also to accept the teacher as an insider in their group.

Creating a need

Before presenting new language, we set up a situation in which the children are searching for that language. The objective is for them to need the language before discovering it. There are a number of ways of creating this need:

Stimulating a question

We mime an animal very quickly, half-draw a picture, hide something or arouse the children's curiosity in some other way. When the children want to ask a question like *What is it?*, *Where is it?* or *What's she doing?* and are searching for a way to express themselves, we help them discover the appropriate English question.

The *How on earth do I say that?!* technique

The children encounter a picture of an egg in a game and they discover how to say *What is it? It's an egg.* They then encounter a picture of an ant in the game. One child asks *What is it?* and another child tries to answer and thinks *How on earth do I say that?!*

When we want to introduce the expression *I don't know*, we ask a child an impossible question, such as *How do you spell soniatarpotalos?* saying the last word very quickly. The child thinks *I don't know!* and wonders *How on earth do I say that?!*

Whatever it is that the children are wondering how to say, we help them discover it in English. The important technique is to make sure that they are searching for the language we want them to learn.

The *How on earth do I say that?!* technique is one of the key methods used in the *Questioning Approach*. In *New Finding Out* Level 1, the way of using it is quite simple, but it can be applied at various degrees of sophistication at all levels of learning.

The *What on earth does that mean?!* technique

We casually slip in the question *How are you?* while we are interacting with one of the children. We don't emphasize this new question. We move on naturally and let her notice this new puzzle, slipping the question in again if necessary. She thinks *What on earth does that mean?!* We want the children to notice the new pattern for themselves and want to discover what it means.

The situation may develop in a number of ways:

1 One of the children may know the answer and the rest of the class can learn from her.
2 We can give a hint so that one of the children can answer.
3 We can encourage the class to ask the question, and they can guess what the question means from our answer.

The first time this technique is used, some of the children may not be sufficiently curious. However, once it has been used a couple of times, the children will recognize the technique and realize how to play the game. They will gradually feel more confident that each mystery will be solved if they risk being curious.

Pausing

Pausing to wonder is an important part of learning. Some approaches to learning, especially those that strongly emphasize physical involvement, neglect the importance of pausing. Some teachers worry when there are pauses in a lesson and hurry to fill in the silence by explaining, moving on to another child too soon or imposing some activity to "get the class going."

When we are creating a need for language, it is essential that we give children space to sense and to wonder. When playing games or practicing language in other ways, they need space to think rather than to just react. (See the notes for Unit 1, **Slam game** for some specific suggestions.)

Solving puzzles

The children should see new language as a series of puzzles. They should solve each puzzle after they have had time to wonder and struggle with it a little, but before they lose interest in it.

When language is presented, a build-up is needed

before the puzzle is solved. We hint and tease the children a little, try to stimulate their interest and then help them discover the solution. Of course, this can be overdone, and we have to consider the time available, but it is important to have some build-up.

Building language

Achievable language

Children make predictions about the new language they encounter based on the patterns and rules that they have sensed. It is essential that a high proportion of these predictions are successful. If new language is not achievable, the children will tend to lose motivation.

The sequence of language in *New Finding Out* has been rigorously tested in class. Each unit follows on from the previous unit in such a way that all language is achievable and no explanation is necessary. If the children find it difficult to make successful predictions about the language in a new unit, it is best to slow down and review for a while.

Linking

To build a secure base from which a child can make predictions with confidence, new language and old language need to be continually linked.

One way of linking is through games. The best games are those that can be used for practicing a wide variety of language at the same time. An example of this is **Car race** (Unit 3), where cards used for practicing different target language can be included in the same racetrack.

Another example of linking can be found in the **Building fluency** sections where children practice switching from one question form to another.

Questioning

Question-answer patterns

When children practice language in sentences (e.g., *It's a cat.*) or as isolated words (e.g., *cat*), it is often difficult for them to produce the language in communicative situations. In *New Finding Out*, vocabulary and structures are often practiced in question-answer patterns (e.g., *What is it? It's a cat.*). Asking and answering questions forms the basis of communicative interaction between people. When

children continually practice language in question-answer patterns, it becomes second nature for them to see language in these terms.

When practicing speaking, one child may ask another child, half the class may ask the other half or the whole class may ask an individual child. The children need many opportunities to practice new vocabulary and structures in question-answer patterns until they are able to produce the language spontaneously and seem unlikely to forget it. It will then become unnecessary for them to ask the question so often, especially if they are likely to do so without feeling or curiosity. If this happens, it is better to switch to practicing the language in sentences for a while, e.g., *It's a cat.*

When practicing writing vocabulary or structures, the children are generally shown some flashcards by the teacher, and they then write a question and answer about each card. (See *Reading and writing*, page 29.)

Negative-answer technique

Compare the following:

a	Teacher	*What is it?*
	Child	*It's a cat.*
b	Teacher	*Is it a cat?*
	Child	*Yes, it is.*
c	Teacher	*Is it a dog?*
	Child A	*No, it isn't.*
	Child B	*What is it?*
	Child A	*It's a cat.*

In **a** and **b**, the teacher is at the center of the conversation and talking as much or more than the children. The conversation also does not lead anywhere. In **c**, the teacher is beginning to move away from the center.

The "negative-answer" technique can be developed in three stages.

1st stage   At this stage, the teacher asks the initial question (e.g., *Is it a dog?*) and the dialogue is continued by the class.

2nd stage	The second stage might look like this:
Child A	*Is it a hippopotamus?*
Child B	*No, it isn't.*
Child A	*What is it?*
Child B	*It's a cat.*

The teacher may be holding the cards and giving hints but doing no more than this. If the children are practicing in pairs, they hold the cards and the teacher helps only when absolutely necessary. We just give hints when necessary and perhaps encourage the children to think of absurd starting questions that make the other children smile – for example, if the picture is a pen, the children may ask *Is it a carrot?* or if the picture is a cow, the question might be *Is it an ant?*

3rd stage   The third stage is usually difficult for the children at first, but it's important to move on to this stage when we feel the children are ready.

After learning the pattern *What does she do?*

Child A	*Is she a boxer?*
Child B	*No, she isn't.*
Child A	*What does she do?*
Child B	*She's a tennis player.*
Child A	*What do you do?*
Child B	*I'm a student.*

At this stage, the emphasis is on making the structure feel more real to the children. The children play around with the patterns and then personalize them.

Concentration

Switching

A lesson consists of a series of activities. There is a limit to how long the children can concentrate on one activity and the idea is to switch to another activity before the children lose concentration and interest. Children will learn a language target more deeply by sometimes switching away from the target during a lesson and then coming back rather than by continually practicing the target itself.

The pace of a lesson

Lessons should always move at a fast, stimulating pace to maintain the children's interest. Establishing this pace in the first lesson encourages the children to regard it as normal.

The pace and the constant switching ensure that the children do not lose concentration and reduce behavior problems. However, as has been stressed before, this does not mean that the children are not given time to pause and think.

Retention

Many children learn English for only one or two hours a week. Under these circumstances, it may seem difficult for them to learn to speak, read and write the language. A key consideration of any course designed for this kind of situation must be how to increase the retention of language that is learned in class.

Review

It is easy for the children to forget what they learned even two or three months previously. All targets need to be reviewed again and again, and new language should be linked with as many of these previous targets as possible. If English is presented as a series of independent language targets, there will be little retention.

The balance of skills

A new target is more likely to be retained if it is approached from a number of different directions. If it is only spoken, it is isolated and difficult for the child to link with previous targets. If it is spoken, read and written, it is much more secure. In *New Finding Out*, the balance of skills is emphasized. Ideally, all target language should be spoken, read and written at an equal level. Writing is usually the most difficult skill to learn. Sometimes it may be necessary to concentrate mainly on writing for a while until it has been brought up to the same level as speaking and reading.

The Home Book and My CD

When children have little time to learn English in class, it is essential to assign them regular homework. The Home Book has been designed for this purpose. It reinforces the targets of the course and concentrates on the most difficult skill – writing. My CD can also make a big difference in how much of the target language is retained.

Pronunciation

Association

The pronunciation of individual letters and letter combinations is learned by associating them with pictures. For example, the letter **Aa** is not pronounced as in **ABC** but as in **apple**. There is a flashcard for the letter **Aa** with a picture of an apple on the back. The letter is generally referred to as *a- apple* and the pronunciation is remembered by association. It is sometimes preferable to use the short form **a** (as in **apple**), particularly with older children or to save time.

Consonants are learned in the same way. The letter **Bb** is pronounced *buh* and referred to as *b- book*, the sound of the consonant having as little voice as possible. (The amount of voice in the pronunciation will vary from teacher to teacher, but it is important that each teacher is consistent. Those who want a model can use the Class Audio recording.)

Double-letter sounds are learned in exactly the same way. For example, **ee** is either referred to as *ee- tree* or just *ee*.

Pronunciation problems

The children may have particular pronunciation problems such as differentiating between **l** and **r**. Many of these problems cannot be solved quickly, and rather than making an issue of the problem at any point, it is better to correct gently over a long period.

Any pronunciation practice should be fun and never mechanical. For example, there is no need to show the children exactly how to shape their mouths when pronouncing a sound or to drill correct pronunciation many times. Pronunciation practice can be accompanied by gestures, facial expressions, imitation of animal noises or anything else that makes the practice fun.

Intonation

When language is practiced many times, there is a danger that intonation may become unnatural. In Level 1 the children may start saying *What is it? It's a …* in a flat and monotonous voice.

When language is first introduced, we should encourage slightly dramatic intonation. In Unit 1 when the children are learning how to say *What is it?*, we should delay leading them toward discovering the answer *It's an ant* until the children really want to know and are asking *What is it?* enthusiastically and with slightly dramatic intonation.

Whether practicing the language as a class, in pairs or in games, the children should always be encouraged to see that using slightly dramatic intonation is fun.

Whose pronunciation?

New Finding Out is designed to be used by teachers of all nationalities.

Native speakers should use their own pronunciation. There will, of course, be a difference between the way something like *o- octopus* is pronounced by American and British teachers, but as long as the pronunciation of each teacher is consistent, there is no problem. Even when the teacher changes, it should not take very long for the children to adjust to different pronunciation.

Non-native speakers can use their own pronunciation or the Class Audio recording as a model.

Humor

The more humor in a lesson, the better. In particular, repetitive practice can be made more fun by using a lot of humor. A few ideas that work well are:

Absurdities

When looking at a picture of a bag, the question *Is it a hippopotamus?* is more fun than *Is it a box?* We can give a few absurd examples and then encourage the children to do the same in pairs.

Mime and gesture

Slightly exaggerated gestures can make the class more fun. For example, hints can be made with gestures, or whenever animals are mentioned the class can mime that animal. The only danger with this kind of method is that we might be too much of an entertainer and become the focal point for the class.

Silly sounds

When children are learning phonics, there are a lot of activities that involve practicing meaningless words. (See *An active approach to phonics*, page 28.) These can be fun. The children can enjoy making new words that sound very silly.

The pace of the course

Momentum

The *Questioning Approach* assumes that when a child learns, she is exploring and moving forward. Learning is a dynamic process.

When using *New Finding Out*, the children should feel that the course is going somewhere. If they stay too long on one target, they may lose motivation. On the other hand, if they move too quickly, they may find new language too difficult and forget what they have already learned. The best approach to adopt is to introduce new language slowly but surely, moving forward and continually linking new language with language the children have already learned.

Flexibility

The language in each unit is learned through a number of activities. These are listed in the guide to each unit later in this book. Some of the activities are optional, and others can be re-used many times. This arrangement allows the teacher to adapt the pace of the course to the needs of individual classes. The amount of classroom time spent on one unit will vary. The teacher may spend only one, or three or four lessons on one unit. Also, the lessons spent on one unit may be interrupted by lessons to review targets from previous units.

When to move on

If the children appear comfortable with the target language that has been learned so far, it is time to move on to the next unit. However, if they are likely to find the new target threatening or if they have forgotten the target of a past unit, it is best not to move on. The target of a new unit should not be presented until it is achievable.

One of the best ways of checking whether the children are ready to move on is by assessing their writing ability. If the target is phonics and they can listen to the phonic sounds and words that contain them and then write them down, they are ready to move on. If the target is a language pattern and they can write personalized sentences or sentences about pictures using that pattern, they are also ready to move on.

4 Games and songs

The value of games and songs

Making learning real

Games play a fundamental role in the lives of children. They tend to see life in terms of games, and anything else is often regarded as something they "have to" rather than want to do. If the children see English as something that "has to" be done and when the class is over they are relieved to be able to run and play with their friends, it is likely that little real learning will take place in the classroom. If learning itself feels like a game and if new language is practiced through games, it is more likely that English will play a central role in the children's world.

Developing a sense for language

Learning is an emotional much more than a rational experience. This is true not only when new language is encountered but also when it is used – sensing how to use the language is more important than rationally understanding how to do so. Games and songs play on the senses. When having fun, the children forget that they are "studying" and acquire language with their senses.

Learning new words and patterns

It is important that the children see games and songs as an integral part of the learning process. Language targets are not "taught" first and then practiced in games and songs. It is the games and songs that motivate the children to want to learn the language targets.

Compare the following:

Traditional method
Teach new language.
Drill until the children can handle the language.
Play a game.

Method used in *New Finding Out*
The children play a game, try to solve a puzzle or sing a song.
They discover new words and patterns inside these games, puzzles and songs.
They engage in more activities where they mix the new words and patterns with others they have learned previously.

Repetition and spontaneity

When children are learning new words and patterns, it is necessary to repeat them many times. Traditionally, this has been achieved through rather dry pattern practice and drills, so spontaneity has generally been lost.

In the method used in *New Finding Out*, spontaneity is maintained because the children never lose their emotional involvement with the language. They learn in fun activities and they practice in fun activities, switching activities before their emotional involvement drops.

Repetition drills outside games are not necessary. The children can repeat language targets far more effectively and naturally inside activities.

For example, **Car race** (full description in Unit 3): Flashcards are laid out in the shape of a racetrack, and the children move cars (or pieces) around the track. The cards may have either the picture side or the written side face up. When the children land on a card, they read it, make a sentence about it, or make a question and answer about it.

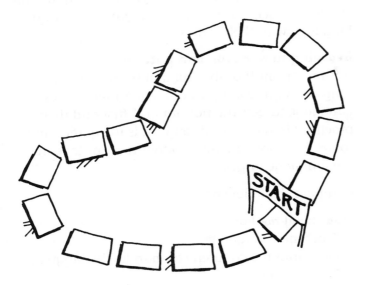

To the children, this is a car race. But it is also a repetition drill. And much more than that, it is a way to learn new words and patterns. As the children get involved in the game, the teacher can casually slip new flashcards into the game. The children land on one of the flashcards and wonder what it is. The extent to which they are emotionally involved in the game affects how much they will

genuinely want to know what the new card is and ask *What is it?* with spontaneity.

Linking language

It has been stressed throughout this introduction that new language must be linked with old language. The most effective way of achieving this is by playing games where more than one target is practiced at the same time.

For example, **Slam game** (full description in Unit 1): Flashcards are spread on the table or floor, the teacher or a child says the name of a card and the children try to touch or slam the appropriate card. After touching the card, the child either identifies what it is, answers a question about it (asked by the rest of the class) or asks and answers the question herself. (See the *Questioning* section in *Advice and techniques*, page 20.)

In the above example, there are single letters to be read, double-letter sounds to be read, and words to elicit the question-answer pattern *What is it? It's a … .* By mixing targets in this way, the children can learn to switch without hesitating from one target to another and so link the language tightly.

The same effect can sometimes be achieved through songs. The **Phonics song** at the end of Level 1 is a good example of this (see Unit 15). In this song, all the double-letter sounds are brought together and practiced flexibly.

Making progress without effort

The best games are generally those that the children enjoy playing and that can be used to practice a wide variety of patterns. If it is found that a class is very fond of a particular game, it can be used many times, but the language content can gradually become more difficult. The children concentrate on playing and trying to win the game and so make progress with little effort.

For example, **Tic-tac-toe** (full description in Unit 2): Flashcards are laid on the table or floor in a square grid, or a grid is drawn on the board. The class is divided into two teams who take turns reading or asking and answering questions about the cards or grid squares. The objective is for one team to complete a whole row successfully before the other team. (For an alternative, see the notes for Unit 2.)

For the version that is drawn on the board, the language content in the game might develop as follows:

Unit 7

1 id	2 t	3 us	4 en
5 at	6 on	7 c	8 v
9 p	10 w	11 ag	12 ib
13 em	14 up	15 ox	16 s

Unit 10

1 It's a frog.	2 dap	3 It's a duck.	4 upad
5 ogin	6 rax	7 mox	8 It's a ring.
9 tib	10 It's a hand.	11 egat	12 bun
13 It's a fox.	14 nid	15 What is it?	16 It's a lemon.

Unit 14

1 armpoy	2 It's a mouse.	3 howtee	4 [ea] seal leaf peach
5 [ee] bee sheep tree	6 seapout	7 It's a shop.	8 shirpee
9 What is it?	10 chipar	11 [ar] car card shark	12 boopoo
13 [ir] girl bird shirt	14 It's a fork.	15 torpoy	16 It's a foot.

Misuse of games and songs

Using them for their own sake
It is important that learning English and having fun are regarded as one and the same thing by the children, so games should be used for practicing language targets. If they are used for their own sake, there is a danger that activities for practicing the target language will seem boring by comparison. In *New Finding Out*, almost all the games and songs are used to practice and link the target language of the course. They are never used to practice language that is unrelated to the course, and, however popular they are, they are never played for their own sake.

Using them to maintain discipline
There is a common tendency to use games and songs as a reward or to maintain discipline – the "If you study hard, we will play a game" approach. This approach can be suicidal – the children gradually come to see learning English as "studying" and playing games or singing songs as "fun," and they lose interest in learning.

Making them too teacher-centered
Some games that are popular are very teacher-centered. An example of this is the traditional way of playing *Bingo* where the teacher says numbers or letters that the children mark off on their individual cards. Before playing any game, a key question to ask is, "How can it be made more child-centered?" In the case of *Bingo*, one child could say the number of a square and all the other children could read what is in that square on their respective Bingo cards.

Using too many of them

The objective is for the children to be stimulated by the language itself, not by switching from one game to another. It is more effective to use the same game quite often, gradually making the language content more difficult, than it is to use a lot of different games. There are many games in *New Finding Out*, but it is not necessary to use all of them. Some will be more suitable for certain children and certain classrooms.

Scoring systems

A good way to make games more interesting is to use a scoring system that the children find fun. Some examples follow.

1 Giving teams names

When the class is divided into teams, each team can be given the name of an animal, a sports team, the team leader or any other name that the children can identify with.

2 Using a sport's scoring system

A game can be scored in the same way as a sport with which the children are familiar. This method can make repetitive practice more enjoyable.

For example, **Baseball**:

The class is divided into two baseball teams and each team is given the name of a baseball team and cutout baseball players or pieces. The batting team has two dice. A baseball field is drawn on a piece of paper.

The teams take turns batting. The first child on the batting team puts her player on home plate and draws a card from the top of the pile. A child from the pitching team asks a question about the card (e.g., *What is it?*) and when the first child answers correctly she moves her piece to first base. There are various ways of proceeding from here:

After answering the question (with the help of her team), the first child rolls the two dice. If she gets a total of 7, she moves her player to first base; if she gets a total of 8, she moves to second base; if she gets a total of 9, she moves to third base; and if she gets 10 or higher, she gets a home run. If she gets less than 7, she is out.

As in real baseball, each team is allowed three "outs" before the turn passes to the other team. If a child gets a hit and would overtake another player from her team, that player moves to the next base. If she gets a home run, she scores for herself and every other player who is on a base. If the pitcher can't think of a question, the batter gets to "walk" to first base.

The scoreboard might look like this:

	1	2	3	4	5	6	7	8	9
frogs	0	1	3						
cows	2	0							

3 Progressive scoring systems

A series of short games can be played (e.g., *Tic-tac-toe*, *Car race*, *Slam game*) and each time a team or individual child wins, her name is moved along a scale.

octopus	frog	rabbit	hippopotamus
Emi			
	Maria		
Akiko			

The objective is to become a hippopotamus. Other headings, such as fruit, objects, or double-letter sounds, could be used instead of animals. The team names could be listed vertically (climbing a ladder) instead of horizontally, and the number of rows or columns can be adjusted according to the game.

Game language

It is a good idea if children can learn game language such as *It's your turn, One point, We won,* and so on. Much of this language can be fed when they use the equivalent expression in their own language.

Making your own games and songs

When making your own games and songs to go along with *New Finding Out*, it may help to consider the following questions and the questionnaire.

Are the children involved?

The more emotionally involved the children feel in a game or song, the more deeply they will learn. If they regard a game or song simply as a classroom exercise, they are unlikely to produce much of the language content spontaneously outside the class. It is also especially important that it is not just two or three of the most active children who feel involved. Is language development integrated?

If the children see getting better at English as a core part of the song or game, we will probably see a lot of highly motivated language learners. This does not mean the children should always be consciously analyzing the language content of an activity as they go along. We want them to play and learn because these two aspects of the activity fit together as seamlessly as possible.

Is active learning encouraged?

From a long-term point of view, one of our biggest responsibilities to the children is to strengthen their natural potential to be self-motivated, active learners. Many teaching methods actually do the opposite. It is so easy for a child to become a passive learner. It only requires a teacher to say *Repeat after me* once too often for the children to not have enough initiative in the games and songs.

Questionnaire

Are the children involved?

1 Would the children enjoy the game or song outside the classroom?
2 Can all the children feel involved?
3 Can those who are weak at English take part without feeling frustrated?
4 Is the song or game clear to understand and use?
5 Does the song or game keep the children's interest until the end?
6 Does the song have a good melody? / Is the game visually stimulating?

Uninvolved								Involved
	-3	-2	-1	0	$+1$	$+2$	$+3$	

Is language development integrated into the game?

1 Can the language content be controlled and focused?
2 Do the children practice English all the time?
3 Do they feel challenged by English?
4 Can new vocabulary be introduced into the song or game?
5 Can new (achievable) structures be introduced into the song or game?
6 Can new language be linked with old language during the song or game?

Language doesn't develop								Language develops
	-3	-2	-1	0	$+1$	$+2$	$+3$	

Does it encourage active learning?

1 How much initiative do the children have?
2 To what extent does the teacher have to explain or demonstrate?
3 How much does the teacher have to do during the song or game?
4 Could the children do any of this?
5 Do the children have opportunities to ask questions?
6 Is new language discovered by the children?

Passive								Active
	-3	-2	-1	0	$+1$	$+2$	$+3$	

5 An active approach to phonics

What is phonics?

In phonics, letters are not pronounced as in ABC, but according to the sound they usually represent – for example, **a** is pronounced as in *apple*. This principle is extended to double-letter sounds (e.g., **ee** is pronounced as in *tree*).

Combining letters

In *New Finding Out*, the children first learn the individual letters and then practice joining them together (from Unit 7). By playing and making mistakes, they learn that sounds are often modified when letters are joined (e.g., **a + t** is not pronounced *atuh* because the final consonant is unvoiced). This kind of rule is never explained; it is discovered. First, two-letter combinations are practiced, then three-letter combinations and then longer words. At each stage, the emphasis is on playing with the letters. The objective is for the children to come to regard any new word they encounter, either to read or write, as a puzzle that looks fun to try to solve. After the children have learned how to join two single letters together, double-letter sounds are introduced and practiced in a similar way.

Sound association

For all children, both those who are familiar with the Roman alphabet and those who are not, phonics can provide a firm foundation in correct pronunciation. The sound association method employed in *New Finding Out* is a particularly effective way of achieving this.

The letter **a** is introduced by a flashcard with **a** on one side and a picture of an apple on the other. The letter is either referred to as *a- apple* or just *a* (as in *apple*). The children remember the pronunciation of **a** by associating it with the word *apple*. The same principle applies to the rest of the alphabet and double-letter sounds: **b** is referred to as *buh- book* or just *buh*; **ee** is referred to as *ee- tree* or just *ee*; and if a combination has two common pronunciations, such as **oo**, these can be distinguished by the words they are associated with, for example, *oo- foot* and *oo- spoon*.

What is distinctive in this approach?

Memorization is minimized

In many approaches to phonics, the children have to memorize difficult letter combinations, such as **ough**, or basic sounds that are not essential to know in the early stages, such as **oi**. In *New Finding Out*, the children only learn a few basic letters and letter combinations, and then they use them to make guesses about how to read or write unfamiliar combinations. The objective is to minimize memorization and maximize use.

Meaningless words are emphasized

If a child can read and write the word *cat* and the word *hat*, it does not necessarily follow that she can read and write the word *bat*, because she may have memorized the first two words. If she can read and write *dat*, *gat* and *yat*, it is likely that she will be able to guess how to read and write *bat* because *dat*, *gat* and *yat* are meaningless, and so she will have had to read them by noticing how the letters combine together and sensing the rhyme, not by memorization.

In *New Finding Out*, patterns and rules for reading and writing are generally established by practicing with meaningless words. The child then uses these patterns and rules to make predictions about new words that may or may not have a meaning. If the new word does have a meaning, the child can be shown a picture or an object to illustrate the meaning of the word. This final stage in the sequence helps the children realize the point of the exercise and gives them a sense of satisfaction.

While practicing meaningless words, the children can enjoy making amusing sounds, inventing their own words and trying to spell sounds that have an interesting meaning in their own language – for example, animal noises and people's names.

Language is natural

Many courses that adopt a phonic approach to reading and writing tend to use unnatural language such as *Pat and Mat sat*. In *New Finding Out*, a lot of trouble has been taken to avoid this. Enough words with irregular spelling have been included to keep the language natural (e.g., in Level 1, *what* is irregular), and the oral-only language is not read or written at this stage, so it does not need to have regular phonic pronunciation.

The emphasis is on building an approach

The main objectives of *New Finding Out* are:

1 To establish a firm base where the English a child knows links together to form patterns that make sense to her.
2 To encourage her to develop a positive and confident attitude toward learning the English she does not know, mainly by strengthening her inquisitiveness and ensuring that her explorations will succeed.

Phonics is used to achieve both of these objectives.

Fear of the unknown

Children who first approach reading and writing through a non-phonic approach have a tendency to distinguish between the words they know and the words they do not know. If they come across a word they have not learned to read or write, many of them will not attempt to read or write it. Some of them are simply afraid of trying, and others do not have any tools to help them. Phonics provides these tools.

The phonic approach makes any word with regular spelling achievable, regardless of how long it is. A child can sight-read words like hippopotamus because she can break them down into their component sounds. The *New Finding Out* approach to phonics convinces her that she can risk trying to read and write them because she believes she will probably succeed.

What about irregular words?

There are a few words that have been introduced as oral-only vocabulary at first, but it is surprising how many of the basic words children need are, in fact, regular. The principle is that children are only expected to read and write irregular words at a rate that does not threaten the basic confidence-building that the course sets out to achieve.

If the child comes to feel that English is written in a way that makes sense, and if her explorations are successful in the early stages, her core approach will be strong enough to handle irregularities in the future. In *New Finding Out*, we are laying the foundations for a positive approach to reading and writing.

6 Reading and writing

Four methods

In *New Finding Out* Level 1, reading and writing are learned through four main methods: phonics, forming sentences, personalized writing and extended reading. The phonic approach has been outlined in the previous chapter.

Forming sentences

Example: Some pictures are placed in a row, possibly along the ledge of the board, and the children write question-answer patterns about each picture. If cards are placed in a row, each child can write at her own speed. For example, the children might write:

1 *What is it?*
 It's a cat.
2 *What is it?*
 It's a cup.

The children can also practice forming sentences in games; for example, one child hides a picture and the other children guess what it is by writing *It's a … , They are …* or *She's -ing* sentences.

Personalized writing

Words and patterns are constantly personalized in games and writing exercises. When a new pattern is encountered, it is not enough to make sentences about Emi or Mark or an animal. The children need to relate it as much as possible to their own lives and their own feelings, and they need to do this when writing just as much as when speaking.

Extended reading

The children move beyond phonics by practicing reading extended passages. They use both phonic and whole-language reading strategies (often with pictures as hints) in order to guess how to read new words. This kind of practice prepares the children to read storybooks with more confidence.

The stages of learning

In *New Finding Out*, reading and writing are learned in the following eight stages:

1 The vowels (Unit 1)
a, e, i, o and *u* are learned from flashcards that have the letter on one side and a picture on the other. The

vowels are generally referred to as *a- apple, e- elephant, i- igloo, o- octopus* and *u- umbrella*. The children learn how to write these vowels by copying and dictation.

2 The consonants (from Unit 2)
Consonants are learned in a similar way to vowels. For example, **c** is pronounced *cuh* and is either referred to as *cuh* or *cuh- cat*. The amount of voice in the sound *cuh* will vary from teacher to teacher and does not matter as long as each teacher is consistent.

3 Two-letter combinations (Unit 7)
A vowel (e.g., *a*) and a consonant (e.g., *t*) are joined together (e.g., *at*) and the children practice pronouncing the combination with the final consonant unvoiced. Many two-letter combinations are practiced.

4 Three-letter combinations (Unit 8)
Three-letter combinations (e.g., *dat, tat, cat*) are practiced in a similar way to two-letter combinations.

5 Long words (Unit 9)
Long words that have regular phonic pronunciation are constructed and decoded. The emphasis is on playing with them and reducing the children's fear of reading and writing them.

6 Question-answer patterns (from Unit 10)
The pattern *What is it? It's a ...* is read and written. A lot of time is spent writing the pattern from picture prompts.

7 Double-letter sounds (from Unit 11)
Double-letter sounds (e.g., *ee*) are introduced and practiced in a similar way to single-letter sounds.

8 Negative-answer patterns (from Unit 13)
The positive answer *Yes, it is* is sometimes practiced, but the main emphasis is on writing the pattern *Is it a ... ?, No, it isn't, What is it? It's a ...* from picture prompts.

From Level 2, the following stages are added.

9 Personalized writing
The children write about themselves, their feelings, their families, famous people they are interested in, animals, and so on, or they make guesses in games using the succession of patterns they encounter in the course.

10 Extended reading
The children read extended passages that contain words they know and words they can guess how to read using phonic patterns, pictures, or general context as clues. These reading passages provide the link between the phonics and patterns learned in the course and the freer language they may encounter when reading storybooks or graded readers. The patterns in these reading passages can also be personalized in writing exercises.

Writing regularly
Writing is the most difficult skill for the children to master and needs to be practiced regularly. Practicing a lot at one time and then not practicing at all for a few lessons seems to be ineffective. Experience shows that there should be a part of each lesson (15–30%) that is devoted to writing.

Most teachers seem to find that writing activities are best left until the end of a lesson and this is what is suggested in the sample lesson plans in this course, but this is not a hard and fast rule. In the first six units of the course, there are also copying activities that should be regarded as additional writing activities and not as a substitute for the writing at the end of the lesson.

Dictation and exercises
The writing part of a lesson is either an exercise or dictation practice. The exercise may be the one in the Class Book, further similar practice in notebooks or extra question-answer pattern practice. The dictation practice may also be the section in the Class Book, further practice in notebooks, or general mixed dictation of any of the target language learned until that point. Letter combinations and sound patterns need to be constantly reviewed.

Neat writing
From the first lesson, it is helpful to encourage neat writing. When the children start writing sentences (in Unit 7), we should check to see that words are evenly spaced, sentences begin with capital letters and punctuation is correct. However, if a child finds this difficult, it is important to be patient and not to expect perfection. We can move on with the course as long as all the children have developed the skill of writing, even if they cannot yet write neatly.

Upper case vs. lower case

At the beginning of the course, the children learn how to read and write both capitals and lower-case letters, but as the course progresses, lower-case letters tend to be emphasized. Most children seem to have little difficulty in learning capital letters and can read them when necessary. When it comes to writing, they learn by trial and error that sentences and some words always begin with capitals.

Minimal prompts

When writing, in the same way as when speaking, prompts should be just enough to lead the child in the desired direction. Just showing the children a picture is generally sufficient to generate a question-answer pattern or negative-answer dialogue.

Hinting and withdrawing

When correcting reading or writing, we hint and withdraw. With reading, the hint might be something like an amusing noise to indicate that there is a mistake. With writing, we can just underline the place where the mistake is and let the child try to discover what it is, giving bigger hints if she is unsuccessful.

Focusing on the vowel

If a child needs more than just a hint to help her read or write a word, the key principle is to focus on a vowel or double-letter sound. If she finds it difficult to read a word like *cat*, we can cover the *c* and the *t* and get the child to read *a*; then we reveal the *t* and the child reads *at*; and finally we reveal the whole word and the child reads *cat*. In some cases, it may be necessary to practice with a few meaningless words to make sure she has recognized the pattern. With writing, the same method can be used, but the letters are dictated instead of read.

7 How to use the guide

The guide to each unit contains classroom activities that are appropriate for introducing and practicing the language in the unit.

The sample lesson plans

At the beginning of each unit guide, there are two sample lesson plans. These plans are intended to illustrate principles and suggest a sequence in which the activities fit together well. They are not intended to be taken literally. An actual lesson plan will depend on many factors such as the length of a lesson, the number of lessons the children have each week, and the age and ability of the children.

A sample plan	
1	Introducing the sounds
2	Goodbye
3	Phonic mime
4	Combining patterns
5	A game or song from a previous unit
6	Introducing the words
7	Writing the letters
8	Home Book preparation

There are two types of activities, shaded and un-shaded.

Shaded activities

These are activities where a multi-skill language target from the unit is being learned or practiced.

These are the activities that really matter. The children's real progress will depend on how well they speak, read and write the language in these activities, not on the language learned in the activities that practice oral-only language targets.

Un-shaded activities

In these activities, an oral-only language target from the current or previous units is learned or practiced, or a multi-skill language target that is completely different from the current unit's multi-skill target is reviewed.

Each un-shaded activity has one or more of the following purposes.

1 To shift the focus of a lesson away from the unit's multi-skill language target for a while

By shifting away from the main language target and coming back to it again, the children will learn the language target faster than if they were to practice it continuously.

2 To provide the children with immediately usable language

Many of the un-shaded activities, particularly the conversation activities, are aimed at satisfying the children's immediate need to communicate and parents' expectations of this.

3 To introduce future multi-skill language targets orally

It often helps if a multi-skill language target is introduced orally some time before it becomes a multi-skill target. For example, *What is it? It's a …* becomes a multi-skill target in Unit 10 but is introduced orally in Unit 1. Other examples are patterns such as *I like …* and *I have …* , which don't become multi-skill targets until later in the course.

4 To review multi-skill language targets that are very different from the current one

The key point about an un-shaded activity is that it should practice language targets that are very different from the language targets being practiced in the shaded activities. At first, all un-shaded activities practice oral-only language targets, but as the course progresses they are increasingly used to review multi-skill targets from earlier in the course.

Planning a lesson

It is important to always have a clear lesson plan. Even for the most experienced teachers, an unplanned lesson is never as good as a planned one. When making the plan, it may help to follow these steps:

1 Decide whether the children are ready to move on

We need to decide which targets from previous units need reviewing and whether the children are ready to move on to a new unit. (See also *When to move on*, page 23.)

2 Decide on the main multi-skill activities

We need to consider which activities are suitable for introducing and/or practicing the main multi-skill target of our lesson. These activities should be planned first and should form the core of the lesson.

3 Decide on the activities that will contrast with the main activities

These activities should be inserted in a lesson at points where you feel the children will need a change.

4 Check to see that the targets are linked

New multi-skill language targets need to be mixed in with old language targets. The children need to link new patterns with old ones and often switch between them. It can be achieved by playing games with flashcards from the current unit mixed with flashcards from previous units. It can also be achieved in any kind of activity where children need to recall words and/or patterns from previous units.

5 Allow time for writing

Writing is the most difficult skill to learn, and it is best learned a little at a time. If a child can just say a language target, you may need to review it again and again. If she can read it, you will need to review it less. If she can write it, she is more likely to move forward and reach her full potential.

6 Allow time for the Home Book

The children should generally be assigned some work from the Home Book to do between each lesson and the next. In each lesson, there needs to be a time to correct the work completed and assigned the new work. (See *The Home Book*, page 14, for specific advice on how to do this.)

Some advice on switching activities

It is best to switch from one activity to another before the children lose interest or concentration. This makes it easier to sustain the children's emotional involvement and makes it more likely that the children will feel positive about the activity if you use it in a future lesson.

When switching away from an activity that practices the main target, it is important that the activity the children switch to is not more enjoyable than the activities for practicing the main target. It is always important to remember to keep the children focused positively on learning the main multi-skill targets.

8 Changes for the new edition

The syllabus

The most popular aspect of the old syllabus has been the way phonics is introduced. This has been kept, strengthened with additional phonics activities and taken much further. In the new syllabus there is a clear progression from phonics to sentences, and from sentences to stories. Children who start the course with no reading and writing skills will be able to read stories and write paragraphs from Level 3.

The new syllabus is also expanded to include many more everyday patterns and vocabulary sets. The vocabulary includes, for example, classroom objects, days of the week and months of the year in Level 1, while the additional patterns in the same level include *I like …* and *I have …* A contents chart can be found on page 3 of each Class Book, with more details on pages 4–5 of the Teacher's Book.

The Class Book

New pages

The new Class Book has expanded, with two new pages in every unit. A full list of activities is given on page 13; this section focuses on the new activity types.

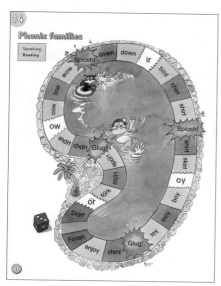

Phonic families (Levels 1–5)

In these activities children play games and learn new words and patterns they will encounter again in the word sets, songs and reading passages. This provides an opportunity for the children to learn

words that are phonically irregular as well as those that are regular.

Words in action pages (Level 1–5)

Each of these pages provides two straightforward communicative activities that give children the opportunity to practice and personalize useful new words and patterns. These pages present useful conversation patterns that may not be phonically regular without compromising the integrity of the *Finding Out* approach. They do this by introducing the new language through child-centered activities, in which children initially only speak and hear the language, and are not expected to read and write it.

Word set pages (Levels 1–5)

On these pages new words are introduced in sets such as fruit, things in the room, cities, and so on. This makes it possible for the children to learn common vocabulary that was omitted from the old syllabus. The language is introduced orally at first, and the vocabulary is linked to the rest of the unit. In lower levels, the link is usually with a Words in action page, whereas in later levels it may also be linked to a reading text or a song.

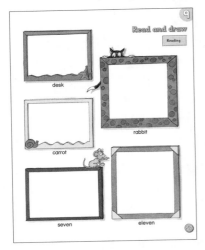

Listen / Read and draw (Level 1) / Color and write (Level 2)

These pages, which all have a similar format, encourage children to respond creatively and through language to a variety of stimuli. These stimuli develop in complexity from basic aural activities (Listen and draw) from the beginning of Level 1, to written text (Read and draw) towards the end of Level 1. In Level 2, children use a visual stimulus to discover and write new words (Color and write).

Building reading skills (Level 2) / Children like us (Levels 3–5)

These reading texts enable children to progress from using phonics into reading stories. They combine patterns children have learned with new words that children can discover using their phonics skills. The range of skills they promote encourages children to approach unknown texts and writing activities with confidence.

In the Children like us activities, children also discover information about different countries and cultures, and similarities between themselves and children elsewhere in the world.

Forming sentences pages (Levels 3–5)

These pages are similar in format to the Word set pages in lower levels. Here, though, the emphasis is on having children discover patterns in the language, and enabling them to personalize these. Where appropriate, children can discover by reading, as well as through the illustrations. In addition to these new page types, there is now a Game in every unit. There are also more Action song pages in the new edition. The new title "Action song" draws attention to the suggestions given in the Teacher's Book for reinforcing the language practiced in the song with actions, and thereby creating a multi-sensory environment for the children.

New design

The Class Book has been redesigned to make it easier for teachers to use.

Each page shows what skills areas are involved in the panel in the top corner, indicating at a glance what language is learned orally and what is multi-skill (i.e. intended to be read and written as well as spoken).

At the beginning of each Class Book there is also a table of contents (page 3), showing the language learned in that level and divided into key multi-skill targets and supplementary language.

There is also an introduction to the activity types in that level (page 4), which will be particularly useful for teachers unfamiliar with the course. It introduces each activity type and briefly explains the goal of the activity.

New CD

For the new edition, each Class Book is packaged with My CD, a free audio CD that children can take home and listen to for pleasure.

The Home Book

The Home Book has also been redesigned to make it easier to use. Each new activity type has text instructions in a panel at the bottom, which provide an easy reference for the teacher or the child's parent or caregiver.

Some pages in Home Book 2 have also been changed to provide practice of "silent *e*" patterns, introduced in Class Book 2.

The Teacher's Book
New design

The Teacher's Book has been completely re-designed and expanded to make it a key resource, particularly for inexperienced teachers. Teaching notes are accompanied by facsimiles of the Class Book and Home Book pages, making it easy to navigate. Games appear in a panel, so that they easy to recognize, and games and songs are also listed in the full scope and sequence on pages 4–5 of each Teacher's Book.

New content

The Introduction, with its comprehensive but straightforward explanation of the *Questioning Approach* (on which *New Finding Out* is based), condenses many years' experience teaching children and training teachers of children in Asia, and provides a wealth of advice and suggestions for any teacher. It has been updated for the new edition. Every activity in the Class Book, including the new pages, is explained with simple step-by-step instructions. Teaching tips are included for those with less experience of the approach, and variations for new and old teachers alike.

All the photocopiable resources needed for the Class Book (including the new activities) are included in the back of the Teacher's Book.

New CD-ROM

Each Teacher's Book is supplemented with a free CD-ROM, containing extra resources for classroom activities, course management and teacher development. See *The Teacher's CD-ROM*, on page 15, for more details.

The Class Audio

The audio component for the new edition is now available as a CD. It contains all the listening material from the old edition, along with support for the new activities and all the new songs.

The Flashcards

The popular flashcards have been repackaged for the new edition, and additional flashcards added in Level 2 to accompany the introduction of "silent *e*" in the Class Book.

A sample plan for the first lesson	A sample plan for a follow-up lesson
1 Introducing the sounds	1 Game – *Basketball*
2 *What's your name?*	2 *What's your name?*
3 Phonic mime	3 Listen and draw
4 Introducing the words	4 Game – *Slam game* (vocabulary cards)
5 Game – *Slam game*	5 *a-e-i-o-u song*
6 *What's your name?*	6 Exercise
7 Writing the letters	7 Dictation
8 Home Book preparation	8 Home Book preparation

See How to use the guide, *page 33, for an explanation of sample lesson plans and shading.*

Phonics

Introducing the sounds

Equipment: Aa, Ee, Ii, Oo, Uu alphabet cards. Class Book page 5. Class Audio (optional).

1 Either hold up the **Aa** card, look at it curiously and smile, or hide it behind something (for example, a book, a toy or your back) and slowly reveal it to the children. If the children are wondering what the letter is and possibly making suggestions but can't or don't say the sound of the letter (e.g., saying *A* as it is pronounced in ABC), say *a* (as it is pronounced in the word apple). Encourage the children to say this with you. They should feel that they are discovering this with you, not saying it after you.

2 Either show the children the apple on the other side of the card, encourage one of the children to turn it over, hide the picture and slowly reveal it or gradually draw a picture of an apple. If the children can't guess what to say, say *apple* with them. The objective is for them to feel that both they and you are discovering something together.

3 Turn back to the letter **Aa** and encourage the children to practice saying *a- apple* a little. From now on, the letter is either referred to as *a- apple* or *a* (as in apple). The children remember how to pronounce **Aa** by associating it with the first sound in the word apple.

4 Do the same for the other letters: **Ee** is either referred to as *e- elephant* or just *e* (as in elephant), **Ii** as **i- igloo** or just *i*, **Oo** as *o- octopus* or just *o*, and **Uu** as *u- umbrella* or just *u*. Then mix the letters and practice them in a random order.

5 Open Class Books to page 5. Appear fascinated by the page. Let the children guess what is happening. If the children don't or can't say the letter on the page, point to the letter **Aa** and indicate that the children should do the same. All the children say *a- apple* together. Continue with the other letters.

Option: Play the recording for model pronunciation.

Phonic mime

1 Mime eating an apple, and encourage the children to guess the sound you are thinking of. You could give them a hint by suggesting *e- elephant*? If they don't say *a- apple* themselves, help them say this.

2 See if the children can figure out mimes for **Ee, Ii, Oo** and **Uu.** If they need help, do your own mimes for letters they can't think of mimes for, such as miming an elephant's trunk for **Ee**, indicating the shape of an igloo with your hands and shivering for **Ii**, eating on orange with juice squirting into your eye for **Oo**, and putting up an umbrella for **Uu**.

3 These mimes can sometimes be used from now when the children are saying the sound of a letter, or as hints when the children are trying to spell a word.

Writing the letters

Equipment: Notebooks.

1 Write **A** on the board, saying the sound and/or miming eating an apple as you do so. Then quickly erase it with a playful grin. The children try to write the letter in their notebooks. (If the class is small, they can write on the board with you.)

2 Write **A** again a bit more slowly, stroke by stroke, and then quickly erase it. You may need to do this more than once.

3 Do the same for **a**.

4 Get one of the children to write **Aa** on the board. You can hint by drawing one or both of the letters in the air with your finger. All the children then write **Aa** a few times in their notebooks.

Repeat this procedure for each of the other letters.

Home Book

The Home Book pages can be completed at any point between here and the end of the unit. Before being asked to do any of the exercises in the Home Book, children should be shown exactly what they are expected to do.

Children write the letters as neatly as possible.

Children write the letters as neatly as possible.

Children write the letter **Uu**. They then match each flag to the thing that begins with that letter.

Children write the starting letter next to each picture.

Conversation

What's your name?

**Equipment: Class Book page 6.
Class Audio (optional).**

1 Look at a child, smile and say *Hello. What's your name?* If she cannot answer, smile again and ask other children. Aim to generate the feeling, "Here is an interesting puzzle to be solved. Trying to solve it could be fun."

Either 2a If nobody can answer, point to yourself and get the children to ask you the question. Tease them a little and don't answer until they really want to know, answer *I'm …* and then ask the question to one or two of the children.

Or 2b If anybody successfully answers the question, see if the other children can use her answer to figure out their own answers.

3 One child asks another in a chain around the class. As they do so, they shake hands. At this stage, it is important that none of the children feel any pressure from having to speak English in front of the class, so help when necessary.

4 Open Class Books to page 6. Let the children look at the picture and guess what is happening.

Option: Play the recording.

> **Teaching tip**: In 2a, after answering *I'm (David)* and then saying *Hello. What's your name?* to a child, she may answer *I'm (David)*. If this happens, you can point to yourself playfully and say *I'm (David)!* and then point to the child and say naturally *What's your name?* If necessary, you could pretend to look for her name in the class roll.

Phonic words

Introducing the words

Equipment: Octopus, egg, ant and album vocabulary cards. These cards can be supplemented with real objects or toys.

1 Use the picture of an ant or one of the other cards you think students will not know in English. Hide the picture and slowly reveal it or gradually draw a picture of an ant. Stimulate the children's curiosity, and when they really want to know what the picture is in English, empathize with their feeling and help them say *What is it?*

2 Pretend you can't hear, or tease them a little in another way, when they ask you the question, so as to get them to ask you again.

3 Discover the answer with them: *It's an ant.*

4 Get the children to slowly reveal other cards or draw pictures of the things on the cards to stimulate them to ask and answer the question *What is it?* among themselves. Help with either the question or answers when necessary.

5 The children play a simple game such as the *Slam game* with the vocabulary cards.

6 Open Class Books to page 6. The children ask and answer *What is it? It's an …* about the pictures.

Game

Basketball

Equipment: Class Book page 7. Aa, Ee, Ii, Oo, Uu alphabet cards, a large die, a basket or box.

1 Open Class Books to page 7. Appear fascinated by the page. Let the children guess what is happening.

2 Divide the class into two or more teams.

3 Either you or one of the children holds up one of the alphabet cards. A child from one team reads the phonic sound aloud. She then tries to throw the die into the basket or box.

4 If the die goes into the basket or box, she gets 10 points. If she misses, she gets the points on the die.

5 Repeat the procedure with the next team. The basket or box can be equidistant from each team or moved around the class in order to help a team that has fewer points or a child who is not as good at throwing.

Variations: Children can do a mime for the letter on the card (e.g., mime eating an apple for **Aa**) and say what the sound is. Children can guess what a hidden card is.

Note: This game can be used throughout the course for just about any language target. The children can say or read a sound, word or sentence or perform any other language task before throwing the die.

Teaching tip: In a very large class, there can be a number of teams. In formal large class with chairs arranged in rows, each row of children can be a team; in a one-to-one lesson, the teacher can be one team.

Listen and draw

**Equipment: Class Book page 8.
Class Audio (optional).**

1 Open Class Books to page 8. Look at the page as if you are wondering what to do, and encourage the children to show you. If this does not work, pick up a pencil, hesitate as if you are wondering what to write and draw, and ask the children for help.

2 If the children don't understand what to do, help them write **Aa** and draw an apple for the first picture frame.

3 Either you, an animal puppet, one of the children, or the children in teams dictate *e, i, o, u* in turn and the children write **Ee, Ii, Oo, Uu** and draw an elephant, an igloo, an octopus and an umbrella.

Option: The children can listen to the recording and write the sounds.

Action song

a-e-i-o-u

Equipment: Class Book page 9. A ball, stuffed animal or puppet (optional). Class Audio (optional).

1 Open Class Books to page 9. Hum the tune, play it on a musical instrument or play the recording.

2 Write the letter **a** on the board, sing *a* (as in apple) and clap. Get the children to do this with you.

3 Continue writing the other letters and see if the children can sing as they read and figure out that they should clap with each sound. If not, help them.

4 Continue in the same way for the first three lines.

5 Don't write "Hello. What's your name?" on the board. After the children sing this line, point to one of the children either with your finger or with a stuffed animal or puppet, or throw a ball or stuffed animal to a child. The child answers *I'm … .*

6 In the second verse, *u* is omitted from the first three lines, in the third verse *o* and *u* are omitted, and so on. The child who answered the question in the first verse chooses who should answer the question in the second verse, and so on.

Variations: The vowels can later be changed to consonants, double-letter sounds or letter combinations. These can either be read from the board, or read one by one from flashcards in order to make the reading less predictable.

The question can later be changed to *How old are you?*, *Where do you live?*, and so on. Alternatively, the recording can be paused and the children can ask and answer a few questions.

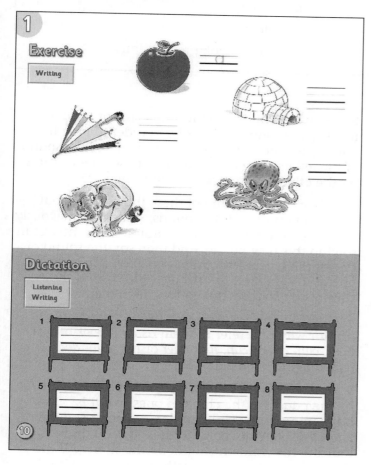

Exercise

Equipment: Class Book page 10. Notebooks. Alphabet and vocabulary cards.

1 Open Class Books to page 10. Look at the Exercise section as if you are wondering how to do it and encourage the children to show you. If this does not work, point to the picture of an apple, say *a* with the children and get them to write the letter. They write the other letters by themselves.

2 Open notebooks. The children write the starting letter of each picture on the cards that you or one of the children holds up. Mix in vocabulary card pictures.

Dictation

Equipment: Class Book page 10. Notebooks. Class Audio (optional).

1 Open Class Books to page 10. Hold up a Class Book and point to each house in the Dictation section in turn. As you point to a house, dictate gently or play the recording:

   a- apple
   o- octopus
   i- igloo
   e- elephant
   u- umbrella
   o- octopus
   i- igloo
   u- umbrella

Repeat each letter as many times as is necessary.

2 If necessary, the children can do more of the same kind of practice in their notebooks.

A sample plan for the first lesson

1 Introducing the sounds
2 *What's your name?*
3 Phonic mime
4 1–12
5 Game – *Basketball* or *Slam game*
6 Introducing the words
7 Writing the letters
8 Home Book preparation

A sample plan for a follow-up lesson

1 Game – *Tic-tac-toe*
2 1–12
3 Listen and draw
4 Game – *a and an game*
5 *Numbers song*
6 Exercise
7 Dictation
8 Home Book preparation

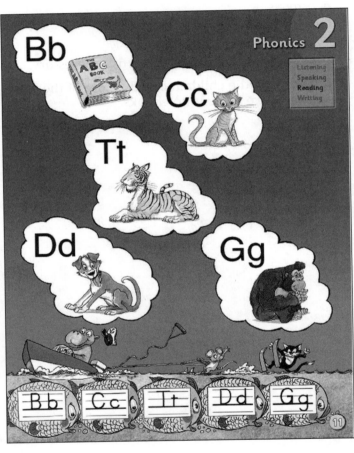

Phonics

Introducing the sounds

Equipment: Class Book page 11. Bb, Cc, Tt, Dd, Gg alphabet cards and the alphabet cards from Unit 1. Class Audio (optional).

1 Play the *Slam game* or *Basketball* using the alphabet cards from Unit 1. When the children are focused on the game, innocently slip one or two of the new alphabet cards into the game and step back.

2 When the children notice the cards or need to identify the sound they make in order to play the game, give them a chance to try to guess the sound of the letters, turn over the cards to see the pictures on the other side or ask you what they are.

3 If they do not do any of these things or try but cannot guess one of the sounds, smile mischievously or look puzzled in order to stimulate their interest in solving this new puzzle, and then say the sound of one of the letters with them (e.g., *buh*). Encourage one of the children to turn over the card. If they cannot say *book* by themselves, help them.

4 The children discover each of the sounds in a similar way and refer to them as *buh- book* or just *buh* , *cuh- cat* or *cuh*, *tuh- tiger* or *tuh*, *duh- dog* or *duh*, and *guh- gorilla* or *guh*.

5 Open Class Books to page 11. Appear fascinated by the page. Let the children guess what is happening. If the children don't or can't say the letter on the page, point to the letter **Bb** and indicate the children should do the same. All the children say *buh- book* together. Continue with the other letters.

Option: Play the recording for model pronunciation.

Teaching tip: This way of introducing sounds works most effectively if a class really likes a particular game, so it is best to choose a game they have shown they like in a previous lesson. It is also best to stop playing the game before the children want to, so that they will be just as positive about the game in the future if you use it to introduce other language targets.

Variation on the first three steps suggested above:
1 Either hold up the **Bb** card, look at it curiously and smile, or hide it behind something (e.g., a book, a toy or your back) and slowly reveal it to the

children. If the children are wondering what the letter is and possibly making suggestions but can't or don't say the sound of the letter, say *buh*. Encourage the children to say this with you. They should feel that they are discovering this with you, not saying it after you.

2 Either show the children the book on the other side of the card, encourage one of the children to turn it over, hide the picture and slowly reveal it or gradually draw a picture of a book. If the children can't guess what to say, say *book* with them. The objective is for them to feel that both they and you are discovering something together.

3 Turn back to the letter **Bb** and encourage the children to practice saying *buh- book* a little.

Phonic mime

1 Mime reading a book and encourage the children to guess the sound you are thinking of. You could give them a hint by suggesting *g- gorilla*? If they don't say *buh- book* themselves, help them say this.

2 See if the children can figure out mimes for **Cc**, **Tt**, **Dd** and **Gg**. If they need help, do your own mimes for letters they can't think of mimes for, such as pulling on an imaginary cat's whiskers or saying *meow* for **Cc**, growling like a tiger for **Tt**, wagging a tail or barking for **Dd**, and banging your fists on your chest for **Gg**.

3 These mimes can sometimes be used from now on when the children are saying the sound of a letter, or as hints when the children are trying to spell a word.

Writing the letters

Equipment: Notebooks.

1 Write **B** on the board, saying the sound and/or miming reading a book as you do so. Then quickly erase it with a playful grin. The children try to write the letter in their notebooks. (If the class is small, they can write on the board with you.)

2 Write **B** again a bit more slowly, stroke by stroke, and then quickly erase it.

3 Do the same for **b**.

4 Get one of the children to write **Bb** on the board. You can hint by drawing one or both of the letters in the air with your finger. All the children then write **Bb** a few times in their notebooks.

Repeat this procedure for each of the other letters.

Home Book

The Home Book pages can be completed at any point between here and the end of the unit. Before being asked to do any of the exercises in the Home Book, children should be shown exactly what they are expected to do.

Children write the letters as neatly as possible.

Children write the letters as neatly as possible.

Children write the letter **Gg**. They then match each cowboy to the thing that begins with that letter.

Children write the starting letter next to each picture.

Numbers

1–12

Equipment: Class Book page 12. A soft ball. **Numbers 1 to 12 (see pages 127–128 or Teacher's CD-ROM). Class Audio (optional).**

1 Hold up the number 1. The whole class says *one* together. Repeat for 2 and 3.

2 Say and mime *Please stand up*. Gesture that you are going to throw the ball to one of the children and get the children to say *one* with you.

3 Indicate that the child who has the ball should throw it to somebody else. The whole class says *two*. Repeat for *three*.

4 Before throwing the ball again, the children will wonder how to say 4. If some of them know, let them learn from each other. If nobody knows, say the number with them as the ball is thrown. Continue for the numbers 5 to 12.

5 Consolidate by holding up the numbers 1 to 12 and getting the children to say them.

6 Open Class Books to page 12. Let the children look at the picture and guess what is happening.

Option: Play the recording.

> **Teaching tip:** Throwing a ball is a useful way to learn and practice many words and patterns. The children can learn sequences such as numbers or days of the week, categories such as vegetables or colors, patterns such as *I like …* or *I can …*; tell stories with each child adding a sentence; and so on. In fact, there are endless possibilities.

Phonic words

Introducing the words

Equipment: Class Book page 12. Bed, dog, bat, tent, bag, cat vocabulary cards and the vocabulary cards from Unit 1. These cards can be supplemented with real objects or toys.

1 Hide one of the new pictures and slowly reveal it or gradually draw a picture of it. If the children don't say *What is it?* with genuine curiosity, continue slowly revealing or drawing the picture, and, if necessary, finally help them say *What is it?*

2 When they ask you the question, pretend you can't hear or tease them a little in another way, in order to get them to ask you again.

3 Discover the answer with them: *It's a (bed)*.

4 Get the children to reveal other cards slowly or draw pictures of the things on the cards to stimulate them to ask and answer the question *What is it?* among themselves. Help with either the question or answers when necessary.

5 The children play a simple game such as the *Slam game* or *Basketball* with the vocabulary cards from this unit mixed up with the cards from Unit 1.

6 Open Class Books to page 12. The children ask and answer *What is it? It's a …* about the pictures.

Tic-tac-toe

Game

Tic-tac-toe

Equipment: Class Book page 13. The alphabet cards learned so far.

1 Open Class Books to page 13. Appear fascinated by the page. Let the children guess what is happening.

2 Close Class Books. Divide the class into two teams. Each team can be given a name.

3 Either you or the children place nine alphabet cards on a table, desk or floor in a 3 x 3 grid with the letters face up. (If the class is large, a grid can be drawn on the board and letters written in each square.)

4 The first child on one team points to any card and tries to say what it is (e.g., *cuh- cat*). If she is correct, the whole team repeats what she said and the card is turned over. The first child on the other team then chooses another card that hasn't been turned over and tries to say what it is.

5 The correct cards for one team are turned over and placed horizontally in the same space in the grid, and the correct cards for the other team are turned over and placed vertically.

6 The game continues. The second child on one team tries, then the second child on the other team, and so on. The winner is the first team to get three cards in a straight line, horizontally, vertically or diagonally.

Variations: The game can be repeated with the pictures face up instead of the letters. In other words, the child points to the picture of a cat and says *cuh- cat*.

4 x 4 or 5 x 5 grids can be used, in which case it is probably best to give one point for any three cards in a straight line, rather than expect teams to complete whole rows or columns.

Variations of the game can be played throughout the course.

Teaching tip: *Tic-tac-toe* can be used for individual phonic sounds, phonic families, saying or reading vocabulary, and saying or reading almost any sentence pattern. When the game is used for vocabulary or sentence patterns, it is often useful to practice questions as well as answers. One child can choose a card and the rest of her team can ask her an appropriate question about the card before she answers and turns over the card.

Game

a and *an* game

Equipment: The vocabulary cards learned so far. Two pieces of paper. A puppet or stuffed animal.

1 The children draw a large **a** and a large **an** on separate pieces of paper and place them on the table or floor. The **a** and **an** can be inside amusing animal shapes.

2 One child has a pile of cards and the other children are in two teams. The child with the cards reveals the top one, and one child from each team races to touch either **a** or **an**.

3 The first child to touch the correct paper gets a point for her team, provided that she says *It's a …* or *It's an …* correctly. If she makes a mistake, the child on the other team is offered a chance to make the correct sentence.

4 The puppet or stuffed animal is the referee. When a child makes a mistake, the animal can make fun noises such as "Uh-oh."

Teaching tip: It is not a good idea to dwell too much on the difference between **a** and **an**. At this stage, the children just need to know that there is a difference, and it is helpful if they can discover the rule for themselves. It is best if the game is just played for a short time and then occasionally played in later lessons.

Listen and draw

Equipment: Class Book page 14.
Class Audio (optional).

1 Open Class Books to page 14. Look at the page as if you are wondering what to do and encourage the children to show you. If this does not work, pick up a pencil, hesitate as if you are wondering what to write and draw, and ask the children for help.

2 If the children don't understand what to do, help them write **Tt** and draw a tiger for the first picture frame.

3 Either you, an animal puppet, one of the children, or the children in teams dictate *d, g, c,* and *b* in turn. The children write **Dd, Gg, Cc, Bb** and draw a dog, a gorilla, a cat and a book.

Option: The children can also listen to the recording and write the sounds.

Action song

Numbers

Equipment: Class Book page 15.
Class Audio (optional).

1 Open Class Books to page 15. Hum the tune, play it on a musical instrument or play the recording.

2 The children wag one finger when singing *one*, two fingers when singing *two*, and so on. When they sing *eleven*, they can move ten fingers next to their heads and nod their heads and move their hands up and down at the same time. With *twelve*, they can move ten fingers next to their legs, and jump, swing or sway their legs as well as moving their hands up and down.

Teaching tip: It may help for the children to keep the books open and sing the song while following it in their books. They can close their books as soon as they can sing the song without them.

Variation: The numbers can be varied. One way of doing this is for the children to take turns drawing numbers from a bag or box while singing. When a child draws out a number, this becomes the next number for the whole class to sing.

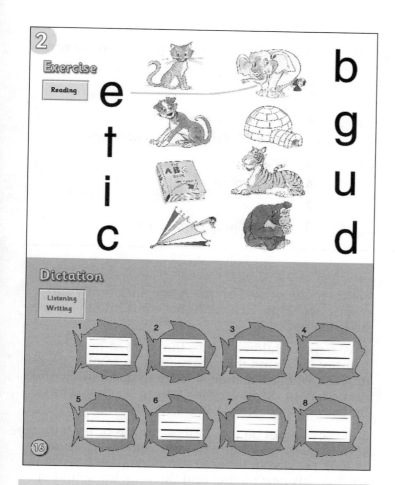

Dictation

Equipment: Class Book page 16. Notebooks. Class Audio (optional).

1 Open Class Books to page 16. Hold up a book, say *one* and point to the first fish in the Dictation section. Put the book down. From now on, say the number of each box before dictating what the children should write.

2 Dictate gently or play the recording:

1 *cuh- cat*
2 *i- igloo*
3 *duh- dog*
4 *tuh- tiger*
5 *guh- gorilla*
6 *u- umbrella*
7 *o- octopus*
8 *buh- book*

Repeat each letter as many times as is necessary.

3 If necessary, the children can do more of the same kind of practice in their notebooks.

Exercise

Equipment: Class Book page 16. Notebooks. Alphabet and vocabulary cards.

1 The children look at pictures on the reverse side of the alphabet cards and say the associated letters. They can do this either individually or as a group.

2 Open Class Books to page 16. Look at the Exercise section as if you are wondering how to do it, and encourage the children to show you. If this does not work, point to the picture of an elephant, say *e* with the children and trace the line from the letter **e** to the elephant with your finger. The children try to match the other letters to the appropriate pictures.

3 Open notebooks. The children write the starting letter of each picture that you or one of the children holds up. Mix in vocabulary card pictures.

A sample plan for the first lesson	A sample plan for a follow-up lesson
1 Introducing the sounds	1 Game – *Car race*
2 1–12	2 *Touch*
3 Phonic mime	3 Combining questions
4 *How old are you?*	4 A game or song from a previous unit
5 A game or song from a previous unit	5 Stretch
6 Introducing the words	6 In the room
7 Writing the letters	7 Exercise
8 Home Book preparation	8 Home Book preparation

Phonics 3

Listening
Speaking
Reading
Writing

Phonics

Introducing the sounds

Equipment: Class Book page 17. Pp, Nn, Mm, Ss alphabet cards and the alphabet cards from previous units. Class Audio (optional).

1 Play the *Slam game*, *Basketball* or *Tic-tac-toe* using the alphabet cards from Units 1 and 2. When the children are focused on the game, innocently slip one or two of the new alphabet cards into the game and step back.

2 When the children notice the cards or need to identify the sound they make in order to play the game, give them a chance to try to guess the sound of the letters, turn over the cards to see the pictures on the other side or ask you what they are.

3 If they do not do any of these things or try but cannot guess one of the sounds, smile mischievously or look puzzled in order to stimulate their interest in solving this new puzzle, and then say the sound of one of the letters with them (e.g., *puh*). Encourage one of the children to turn over the card. If they cannot say *panda* by themselves, help them.

4 The children discover each of the sounds in a similar way and refer to them as *puh- panda* or just *puh, nuh- nut* or *nuh, muh- mouse* or *muh*, and *suh- sock* or *suh*.

5 Open Class Books to page 17. Appear fascinated by the page. Let the children guess what is happening. If the children don't or can't say the letter on the page, point to the letter **Pp** and indicate the children should do the same. All the children say *puh- panda* together. Continue with the other letters.

Option: Play the recording for model pronunciation.

Variation on the first three steps suggested above:
1 Either hold up the **Pp** card, look at it curiously and smile, or hide it behind something (e.g., a book, a toy or your back) and slowly reveal it to the children. If the children are wondering what the letter is and possibly making suggestions but can't or don't say the sound of the letter, say *puh*. Encourage the children to say this with you. They should feel that they are discovering this with you, not saying it after you.

2 Either show the children the panda on the other side of the card, encourage one of the children to turn it over, hide the picture and slowly reveal it or gradually draw a picture of a panda. If the children can't guess what to say, say *panda* with them. The objective is for them to feel that both they and you are discovering something together.

3 Turn back to the letter **Pp** and encourage the children to practice saying *puh- panda* a little.

Phonic mime

1 Mime trying to crack a nut, and encourage the children to guess the sound you are thinking of. You could give them a hint by suggesting *m- mouse*? If they don't say *nuh- nut* themselves, help them say this.

2 See if the children can figure out mimes for **Pp**, **Mm** and **Ss**. If they need help, do your own mimes for letters they can't think of mimes for, such as nibbling on bamboo for **Pp**; scurrying around, moving and then stopping and listening for **Mm**; and putting on a sock for **Ss**.

3 These mimes can sometimes be used from now on when the children are saying the sound of a letter, or as hints when the children are trying to spell a word.

Writing the letters

Equipment: Notebooks.

1 Write **P** on the board, saying the sound and/or miming nibbling on bamboo as you do so. Then quickly erase it with a playful grin. The children try to write the letter in their notebooks. (If the class is small, they can write on the board with you.)

2 Write **P** again a bit more slowly, stroke by stroke, and then quickly erase it.

3 Do the same for **p**.

4 Get one of the children to write **Pp** on the board. You can hint by drawing one or both of the letters in the air with your finger. All the children then write **Pp** a few times in their notebooks.

Repeat this procedure for each of the other letters.

Home Book

The Home Book pages can be completed at any point between here and the end of the unit. Before being asked to do any of the exercises in the Home Book, children should be shown exactly what they are expected to do.

Children write the letters as neatly as possible.

Children write the letters as neatly as possible.

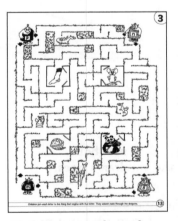

Children match each letter to the thing that begins with that letter. They cannot pass through the dragons.

Children write the starting letter next to each picture.

Combining questions

1 Look at a child and say *Hello. What's your name?* After she answers, say *How old are you?*

2 The children ask these questions quickly, one after the another, in a chain around the class. It is best to vary the chain. If the children don't do this themselves, it can be done by occasionally pointing to the next child to ask.

Phonic words

Introducing the words

Equipment: Class Book page 18. Panda, pot, nut, pin, pen, bus vocabulary cards and vocabulary cards from the previous units. These cards can be supplemented with real objects or toys.

1 Hide one of the new pictures and slowly reveal it or gradually draw a picture of it. If the children don't say *What is it?* with genuine curiosity, continue slowly revealing or drawing the picture, and, if necessary, finally help them say *What is it?*

2 When they ask you the question, pretend you can't hear or tease them a little in another way, in order to get them to ask you again.

3 Discover the answer with them: *It's a (pot).*

4 Get the children to reveal other cards slowly or draw pictures of the things on the cards to stimulate them to ask and answer the question *What is it?* among themselves. Help with either the question or answers when necessary.

5 The children play a simple game such as the *Slam game, Basketball* or *Tic-tac-toe* with the vocabulary cards from this unit mixed up with the cards from Units 1 and 2.

6 Open Class Books to page 18. The children ask and answer *What is it? It's a …* about the pictures.

Conversation

How old are you?

Equipment: Class Book page 18. A soft ball. Number cards for each of the children's ages. Class Audio (optional).

1 The children review the numbers 1 to 12 by throwing the ball around the class and counting.

2 Look at a child, smile and say *How old are you?* If she cannot answer, ask other children.

Either 3a If nobody can answer, show one of the children two cards (one of which is her real age) and suggest what her age might be (e.g., say *Eight? Nine?*). Some of the children will realize that you are asking their age. Help them say *I'm … .*

Or 3b If one of the children successfully answers the question, use her answer as the model for the rest of the class.

3 One child asks another in a chain around the class.

4 Open Class Books to page 18. Let the children look at the picture and guess what is happening.

Option: Play the recording.

Game

Car race

Equipment: Class Book page 19. The alphabet cards learned so far. A small car or piece for each child, brightly colored cards, a starting and finishing line (see page 130 or Teacher's CD-ROM), number cards (see pages 127–129 or Teacher's CD-ROM) or a die.

1 Open Class Books to page 19. Appear fascinated by the page. Let the children guess what is happening.

2 Close Class Books. Place the alphabet cards end to end (letter side up) to resemble a racetrack. Place a few brightly colored cards at irregular intervals along the track.

3 Place starting and finishing lines at a convenient part of the track. If the number cards are being used, place them face down in a pile. Each child chooses a car (or piece) and places it on the starting line. Decide the number of laps.

4 The children draw number cards from the pile or roll a die to decide who goes first. Each child says aloud the number she has drawn or rolled.

5 The child who starts draws a number card, says what the number is, and moves her car around the track; i.e., if she draws a four, she moves her car along four cards. She must say what each letter is that she passes over or lands on (e.g., *a- apple* or just *a*).

6 If the car lands on a brightly colored card, the child has another turn.

7 Crashes. When twelve number cards are used and a 10 or 11 is drawn, the car is considered to have crashed. Instead of moving along the track, the car is placed next to the card it was on. On the next turn, the car is just placed back onto the card again – so one turn is missed. If the track is short, it may be best to use only the number cards from 1 to 6 or roll a die. In either case, the number 3 is a good card to use to indicate a crash.

Variations: This game can be used throughout the course. The cards in the track can be vocabulary cards, occupation cards, action cards, and so on, and can be used for practicing either speaking or reading. Either the child moving her car says or reads the sounds, words or sentences that she passes over with her car, or she answers a question about the cards asked by the other children who are playing.

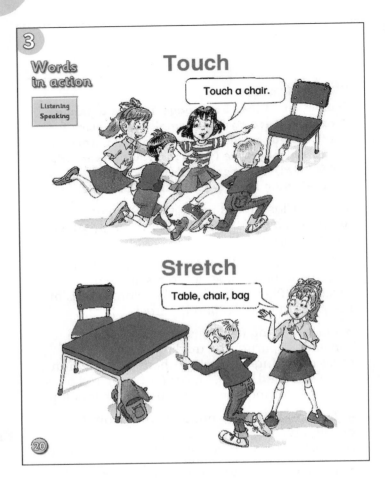

change roles, and Team B tries to touch more objects than Team A. The teams alternate like this. The objective is to create a stronger incentive for the children to ask you about things in the room they don't know in English.

Stretch

Equipment: Class Book page 20.

1 Open Class Books to page 20 and give the children a chance to look at the bottom picture and get a feel for what's happening.

2 One child says the name of something in the room, e.g., *table*. Either the next child in turn, the children on another team or all the other children touch that object.

3 The next child says the name of the object they have just touched followed by another object. The next child, the children on another team or all the other children have to touch both objects in turn.

Teaching tip: The sequence may be difficult to remember after a while, so it is best to encourage all the children or the children on the same team to help the child who is trying to remember it.

Words in action

Touch

Equipment: Class Book page 20.

1 Open Class Books to page 20 and give the children a chance to look at the top picture and get a feel for what's happening.

2 Say *Touch a (bag)!* to one of the children. If she doesn't understand, gesture to the bag and indicate that she should touch it. Help her say *Touch a …* to another child.

3 The children continue to ask each other to touch things. At this stage, they probably don't know the English for many things in the room. The objective is to generate their curiosity to know the English for some of these things. If the children don't ask you spontaneously but are looking at some object they don't know in English, help them ask you *What is it?*, and answer these questions naturally.

Variation: Once the children have gotten the basic idea and learned the English for some of the things they didn't know, they can be divided into teams. Children from Team A take turns saying *Touch …* to other members of the team. Team B counts how many different objects they touch. The teams then

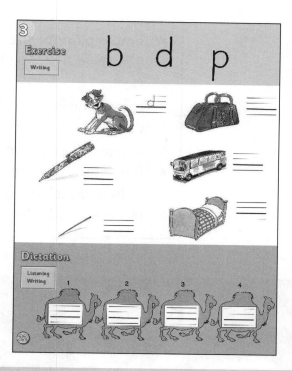

Word set

In the room

Equipment: Class Book page 21. "In the room" picture cards (see page 131 or Teacher's CD-ROM), vocabulary cards from previous units.

1 Open Class Books to page 21. Appear curious about the page as if you are trying to figure out what the things are in English. See if the children can tell you. If you ask *What is it?*, ask as if you are not completely sure or ask with a puppet or stuffed animal that genuinely doesn't know.

2 Play any of the games the children know so far using the "In the room" picture cards mixed up with other vocabulary cards.

Exercise

Equipment: Class Book page 22. The alphabet cards learned so far, alphabet cards and vocabulary cards that begin with b, d or p. Notebooks.

Either 1a Play the *a* and *an* game, but instead of *a* and *an* use three pictures, with **b**, **d** and **p** writen on them.

Or 1b The children look at pictures on the reverse side of the alphabet cards and vocabulary cards. They say the starting letters.

2 Open Class Books to page 22. Point to the picture of a dog, say *duh* and get them to write the letter **d**. They write the other letters by themselves.

3 If necessary, the children can continue with more of the same kind of practice in their notebooks.

Dictation

Equipment: Class Book page 22. Notebooks. Class Audio (optional).

1 Open Class Books to page 22. The children write a letter in each of the camels. Dictate gently or play the recording:

1 buh- book	2 puh- panda
3 duh- dog	4 puh- panda

Repeat each letter as many times as is necessary, avoiding putting any pressure on the children.

2 If necessary, the children can do more of the same kind of practice in their notebooks.

A sample plan for the first lesson

1 Introducing the sounds
2 *I'm fine*
3 Phonic mime
4 Combining questions
5 A game or song from a previous unit
6 Introducing the words
7 Writing the letters
8 Home Book preparation

A sample plan for a follow-up lesson

1 Game – *Car race*
2 Days of the week
3 A game or song from a previous unit
4 *How are you?*
5 Song – *It's Sunday*
6 Exercise
7 Dictation
8 Home Book preparation

Phonics

Introducing the sounds

Equipment: Class Book page 23. Kk, Hh, Qq, Jj alphabet cards and the alphabet cards from previous units. Class Audio (optional).

1 Play one of the games from a previous unit using the alphabet cards from the previous units. When the children are focused on the game, innocently slip one or two of the new alphabet cards into the game and step back.

2 When the children notice the cards or need to identify the sound they make in order to play the game, give them a chance to try to guess the sound of the letters, turn over the cards to see the pictures on the other side or ask you what they are.

3 If they do not do any of these things or try but cannot guess one of the sounds, smile mischievously or look puzzled in order to stimulate their interest in solving this new puzzle, and then say the sound of one of the letters with them (e.g., *huh*). Encourage one of the children to turn over the card. If they cannot say **hat** by themselves, help them.

4 The children discover each of the sounds in a similar way and refer to them as *huh- hat* or just *huh*, *kuh- key* or *kuh*, *juh- jacket* or *juh*, and *kwuh- queen* or *kwuh*.

5 Open Class Books to page 23. Appear fascinated by the page. Let the children guess what is happening. If the children don't or can't say the letter on the page, point to the letter **Hh** and indicate the children should do the same. All the children say *huh- hat* together. Continue with the other letters.

Option: Play the recording for model pronunciation.

Variation on the first three steps suggested above:
1 Either hold up the **Hh** card, look at it curiously and smile, or hide it behind something (e.g., a book, a toy or your back) and slowly reveal it to the children. If the children are wondering what the letter is and possibly making suggestions but can't or don't say the sound of the letter, say *huh*. Encourage the children to say this with you. They should feel that they are discovering this with you, not saying it after you.

2 Either show the children the hat on the other side of the card, encourage one of the children to turn it over, hide the picture and slowly reveal it or gradually draw a picture of a hat. If the children can't guess what to say, say *hat* with them. The objective is for them to feel that both they and you are discovering something together.

3 Turn back to the letter **Hh** and encourage the children to practice saying huh- hat a little.

Phonic mime

1 Mime unlocking a door, and encourage the children to guess the sound you are thinking of. You could give them a hint by suggesting *j- jacket?* If they don't say *kuh- key* themselves, help them say this.

2 See if the children can figure out mimes for **Hh**, **Jj** and **Qq**. If they need help, do your own mimes for letters they can't think of mimes for, such as putting a hat on your head for **Hh**, putting on a jacket for **Jj**, and waving to a crowd and looking regal for **Qq**.

3 These mimes can sometimes be used from now on when the children are saying the sound of a letter, or as hints when the children are trying to spell a word.

Writing the letters

Equipment: Notebooks.

1 Write **H** on the board, saying the sound and/or miming putting on a hat as you do so. Then quickly erase it with a playful grin. The children try to write the letter in their notebooks. (If the class is small, they can write on the board with you.)

2 Write **H** again a bit more slowly, stroke by stroke, and then quickly erase it.

3 Do the same for **h**.

4 Get one of the children to write **Hh** on the board. You can hint by drawing one or both of the letters in the air with your finger. All the children then write **Hh** a few times in their notebooks.

Repeat this procedure for each of the other letters.

Home Book

The Home Book pages can be completed at any point between here and the end of the unit. Before being asked to do any of the exercises in the Home Book, children should be shown exactly what they are expected to do.

Children write the letters as neatly as possible.

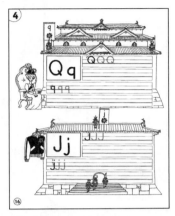

Children write the letters as neatly as possible.

Children match each letter to the thing that begins with that letter. They must cross the river via a bridge.

Children write the starting letter next to each picture.

Conversation

I'm fine

**Equipment: Class Book page 24.
Class Audio (optional).**

1 Look at a child and say *How are you?* If she cannot answer, smile and switch to asking children *What's your name?* or *How old are you?* questions and then casually slip in another *How are you?* question. Grin as if to say, "Here's another puzzle to solve and it's going to be fun."

Either 2a If nobody can answer, point to yourself and get the children to ask you the question. Tease them a little and don't answer until they really want to know. Then smile broadly, exaggerate how fine you feel and say *I'm fine, I'm fine.*

Or 2b If one of the children successfully answers the question, use her answer as the model for the rest of the class.

3 One child asks another in a chain around the class.

4 Open Class Books to page 24. Let the children look at the picture and guess what is happening.

Option: Play the recording.

Combining questions

1 Look at a child and ask her the questions *Hello. What's your name?*, *How are you?* and *How old are you?* in sequence.

2 The children ask these questions quickly, one after another, in a chain around the class. It is best to vary the chain. If the children don't do this themselves, it can be done by occasionally pointing to the next child to ask.

Phonic words

Introducing the words

Equipment: Class Book page 24. Hat, desk, hand, duck, sock, jet vocabulary cards and vocabulary cards from previous units. These cards can be supplemented with real objects or toys.

1 Hide one of the new pictures and slowly reveal it or gradually draw a picture of it. If the children don't say *What is it?* with genuine curiosity, continue slowly revealing or drawing the picture, and, if necessary, finally help them say *What is it?*

2 When they ask you the question, pretend you can't hear or tease them a little in another way, in order to get them to ask you again.

3 Discover the answer with them: *It's a (hand).*

4 Get the children to reveal other cards slowly or draw pictures of the things on the cards, to stimulate them to ask and answer the question *What is it?* among themselves. Help with either the question or answers when necessary.

5 The children play one of the flashcard games from the previous units with the vocabulary cards from this unit mixed up with the cards from previous units.

6 Open Class Books to page 24. The children ask and answer *What is it? It's a …* about the pictures.

Expressions

Equipment: Class Book page 25. Badges of various facial expressions (see page 132 or Teacher's CD-ROM).

1 Copy and cut out the badges. Each child needs a badge, so it may be necessary to make more than one of each type.

2 Open Class Books to page 25. Appear fascinated by the page. Give the children time to guess what is happening.

3 Close Class Books. Pin one badge on yourself and get the children to ask *How are you?* Make an exaggerated facial expression similar to the one on the badge and answer, for example, *Not so good*. The children repeat what you say and try to mimic the facial expression.

4 Each child pins on a badge. They ask each other *How are you?*, either in a chain or walking around the room. When they don't know how to say *Terrible!*, *Great!* or one of the other expressions, help them.

5 The children exchange badges and repeat the activity.

> **Teaching tip**: It is not necessary for each child to use all the badges. The practice should be stopped before the children lose interest. They will have opportunities to practice the other facial expressions when the activity is returned to in later lessons.

6 Say to one child *Hello. How are you?*, *How old are you?* and *How are you?* in sequence. If she doesn't seem to be answering the last question with a genuine answer, suggest possible answers (*Great?*, *Not so good?*, and so on) with exaggerated facial expressions. She gives her own genuine answer with the appropriate exaggerated expression. If she wants to say something very different, such as *I'm hungry*, then help her say it.

7 The children ask each other these three questions, either in a chain or walking around the room.

> **Teaching tip**: From now on, when they are asked the question *How are you?* in class, the children should be encouraged to give a real answer and an exaggerated facial expression to go with it.

Variation: As an extension in the same lesson or a later lesson, the badges can be secretly pinned on the back of each child. Each child walks around trying to find out which badge is on her back. To do so, she goes up to another child who says *How are you?* The child answers *Great?*, and the child asking the question says *Yes* or *No*. If the answer is *No*, the child either continues making guesses or moves on to another child and makes a guess.

4

Words in action

Listening Speaking

Days of the week

Sunday

How are you?

How are you?

26

How are you?

Equipment: Class Book page 26.
  Stuffed animals or puppets.

1 Open Class Books to page 26 and give the children a chance to look at the bottom picture and get a feel for what's happening.

2 One child holds an animal and another child asks the animal *How are you?* The child holding the animal answers with the imagined voice of that animal. The children do this for a number of different stuffed animals.

Teaching tip: One of the purposes of this activity is for animals that may be used in the class on a regular basis to begin to develop characters – for example, an animal that the children see as being lazy might yawn and say *I'm tired*. These animals can become part of the class. One could be the referee awarding points, others can join in games, and all can take part in dialogues in order to make them more fun, and encourage the children to be more creative and spontaneous.

Words in action

Days of the week

Equipment: Class Book page 26.

1 Open Class Books to page 26 and give the children a chance to look at the top picture and get a feel for what's happening.

2 Hit a balloon to a child and say *Sunday!* The objective is for the child to hit the balloon and say *Monday!* She may be able to say this either by herself or with the help of other children. If not, give a hint. One idea is to have a calendar or write a weekly calendar up on the board with dates instead of days of the week, point to the date for Sunday and then point to the next date. When the children want to know what comes after Sunday, help them discover how to say Monday.

3 The game continues in the same way. Once the children get the basic idea, they can just enjoy hitting the balloon around more freely, saying the days of the week in sequence.

Variations: If one child hits the balloon twice, she has to say the same day of the week twice. If the balloon touches the floor or a piece of furniture, the children have to start again from *Sunday*.

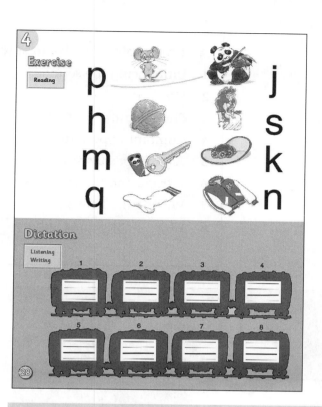

Action song

It's Sunday

Equipment: Class Book page 27. Class Audio.

1 Write these letters on the board: **b d p q h n s**.

2 Open Class Books to page 27 and give the children a chance to look at the picture and get a feel for what's happening.

3 Close Class Books. Play the recording.

4 Play the version without words and see if the children can sing the song. Help when necessary.

5 Encourage the children to do the actions with the song. With the first verse, they rock their arms. With the second verse, they gesture toward other children, and then all or some of the children give genuine answers or act out answers to the question *How are you?* They then read the sequence of letters with phonic pronunciation, first from left to right and then from right to left. Finally, the children sing the last verse with the same gestures as for the first verse, and with some or all of the children giving genuine answers or acting out answers to the question *How are you?*

6 The children figure out a different sequence of letters to read from the board, then sing again, substituting Monday for Sunday and reading the new sequence of letters from left to right, then from right to left.

Exercise

Equipment: Class Book page 28. The alphabet and vocabulary cards learned so far. Notebooks.

1 The children look at pictures on the reverse side of the alphabet cards. They say the associated letters, either individually or as a group.

2 Open Class Books to page 28. Look at the Exercise section as if you are wondering how to do it, and encourage the children to show you. Or point to the picture of a panda, say *puh* and trace a line from the letter **p** to the panda. The children join the other letters to the appropriate pictures.

3 Open notebooks. The children write the starting letter of each picture (use alphabet and vocabulary card pictures) that you or one of the children holds up.

Dictation

Equipment: Class Book page 28. Notebooks. Class Audio (optional).

1 Open Class Books to page 28. The children write a letter in each of the train carriages. Dictate gently or play the recording:

1 huh- hat	2 e- elephant	3 juh- jacket
4 duh- dogk	5 wuh- queen	6 puh- panda
7 kuh- key	8 juh- jacket	

2 If necessary, the children can do more of the same kind of practice in their notebooks.

A sample plan for the first lesson	A sample plan for a follow-up lesson
1 Introducing the sounds	1 Game – *On my head*
2 *Goodbye*	2 *I have …*
3 Phonic mime	3 Practice of the alphabet in a game the children like
4 Combining patterns	4 At home
5 A game or song from a previous unit	5 My things
6 Introducing the words	6 Exercise
7 Writing the letters	7 Dictation
8 Home Book preparation	8 Home Book preparation

Phonics

Introducing the sounds

Equipment: Class Book page 29. Ll, Ww, Ff, Vv alphabet cards and the alphabet cards from previous units. Class Audio (optional).

1 Play one of the games from a previous unit using the alphabet cards from the previous units. When the children are focused on the game, innocently slip one or two of the new alphabet cards into the game and step back.

2 When the children notice the cards or need to identify the sound they make in order to play the game, give them a chance to try to guess the sound of the letters, turn over the cards to see the pictures on the other side or ask you what they are.

3 If they do not do any of these things or try but cannot guess one of the sounds, smile mischievously or look puzzled in order to stimulate their interest in solving this new puzzle, and then say the sound of one of the letters with them (e.g., *luh*). Encourage one of the children to turn over the card. If they cannot say *lion* by themselves, help them.

4 The children discover each of the sounds in a similar way and refer to them as *luh- lion* or just *luh*, *wuh- watch* or *wuh*, *fuh- fish* or *fuh*, and *vuh- violin* or *vuh*.

5 Open Class Books to page 29. Appear fascinated by the page. Let the children guess what is happening. If the children don't or can't say the letter on the page, point to the letter **Ll** and indicate the children should do the same. All the children say *luh- lion* together. Continue with the other letters.

Option: Play the recording for model pronunciation.

Variation on the first three steps suggested above:
1 Either hold up the **Ll** card, look at it curiously and smile, or hide it behind something (e.g., a book, a toy or your back) and slowly reveal it to the children. If the children are wondering what the letter is and possibly making suggestions but can't or don't say the sound of the letter, say *luh*. Encourage the children to say this with you. They should feel that they are discovering this with you, not saying it after you.

2 Either show the children the lion on the other side of the card, encourage one of the children to turn it over, hide the picture and slowly reveal it or gradually draw a picture of a lion. If the children can't guess what to say, say *lion* with them. The objective is for them to feel that both they and you are discovering something together.

3 Turn back to the letter **Ll** and encourage the children to practice saying *luh- lion* a little.

Phonic mime

1 Mime playing a violin, and encourage the children to guess the sound you are thinking of. You could give them a hint by suggesting *fuh- fish?* If they don't say *vuh- violin* themselves, help them say this.

2 See if the children can figure out mimes for **Ll**, **Ww** and **Ff**. If they need help, do your own mimes for letters they can't think of mimes for, such as roaring lion for **Ll**, blowing out your cheeks and swimming for **Ff**, and stretching out your arms to indicate the hands of a watch and moving them slowly while saying *tick tick* for **Ww**.

3 These mimes can sometimes be used from now on when the children are saying the sound of a letter, or as hints when the children are trying to spell a word.

Writing the letters

Equipment: Notebooks.

1 Write **F** on the board, saying the sound and/or miming a fish as you do so. Then quickly erase it with a playful grin. The children try to write the letter in their notebooks. (If the class is small, they can write on the board with you.)

2 Write **F** again a bit more slowly, stroke by stroke, and then quickly erase it.

3 Do the same for **f**.

4 Get one of the children to write **Ff** on the board. You can hint by drawing one or both of the letters in the air with your finger. All the children then write **Ff** a few times in their notebooks.

Repeat this procedure for each of the other letters.

Home Book

The Home Book pages can be completed at any point between here and the end of the unit. Before being asked to do any of the exercises in the Home Book, children should be shown exactly what they are expected to do.

Children write the letters as neatly as possible.

Children write the letters as neatly as possible.

Children match each letter to the thing that begins with that letter.

Children write the starting letter next to each picture.

Conversation

Goodbye

Equipment: Class Book page 30.
Class Audio (optional).

1 Suddenly stop whatever you are doing, go to the door, open it, wave and say *Goodbye*. The more you can surprise the children the better.

2 Wave more and get them to wave, too. Say *Goodbye* and feed the response *See you*.

3 Gesture for one of the children to go to the door. The child says *Goodbye* and the other children say *See you*.

4 Open Class Books to page 30. Let the children guess what is happening.

Option: Play the recording.

> **Teaching tip:** From now on, when appropriate, a child or the teacher leaving the class can wave and say *Goodbye* and the other children wave and say *See you*.

Combining patterns

1 Look at a child and ask her the questions *Hello. What's your name?*, *How are you?* and *How old are you?* in sequence. Then wave and say *Goodbye*. After she has replied *See you*, gesture for her to ask another child the questions.

2 Continue in a chain or get the children to move around the room asking each other questions in any order.

Phonic words

Introducing the words

Equipment: Class Book page 30. Leg, cap, lemon, flag, melon, cup vocabulary cards and vocabulary cards from previous units. These cards can be supplemented with real objects or toys.

1 Hide one of the new pictures and slowly reveal it or gradually draw a picture of it. If the children don't say *What is it?* with genuine curiosity, continue slowly revealing or drawing the picture, and, if necessary, finally help them say *What is it?*

2 When they ask you the question, pretend you can't hear or tease them a little in another way, in order to get them to ask you again.

3 Discover the answer with them: *It's a (flag)*.

4 Get the children to reveal other cards slowly or draw pictures of the things on the cards to stimulate them to ask and answer the question *What is it?* among themselves. Help with either the question or answers when necessary.

5 The children play one of the flashcard games from the previous units with the vocabulary cards from this unit mixed up with the cards from previous units.

6 Open Class Books to page 30. The children ask and answer *What is it? It's a …* about the pictures.

Game

On my head

Equipment: Class Book page 31. The alphabet cards from this unit and previous units.

1 Open Class Books to page 31. Appear fascinated by the page. Give the children time to guess what is happening.

2 Close Class Books. One child in the class or in each group or pair looks at about seven flashcards spread out in front of her. She then puts one or both of her hands on her head.

3 Another child gathers up the cards and secretly puts one of the cards in the hand(s) of the child who has her hand(s) on her head, so that all the children except the child holding the card can see what the card is.

4 The child holding the card on her head tries to guess what the card is, for example by saying *wuh?* or *wuh- watch?* The other children say *Yes* or *No*.

5 The children take turns having cards on their heads.

Teaching tip: If appropriate, there can be a scoring system. For example, if there are seven cards, a child could get seven points for guessing correctly with her first guess, six points for guessing correctly with her second guess, and so on.

Variation: This activity can be used at any stage of *New Finding Out* with almost any flashcards, pictures or words. For example, it could be used with vocabulary cards, adjectives or occupations. It can also be used for cards from a mixture of categories. It can, of course, be used just for speaking when pictures are used, or for reading when sounds, words or sentences are used.

2 Draw a simple picture of a house or apartment, pause and then point to yourself and to the picture and say *My home*. Think for a second, point at the drawing and then say *I have a (computer)*.

3 The children take turns saying things they have at home.

Words in action

I have ...

Equipment: Class Book page 32.

1 Open Class Books to page 32 and give the children a chance to look at the top picture and get a feel for what's happening.

2 Search inside your bag or pocket, pull something out and place the object in front of you. Say *I have a (notebook)*. Gesture for one of the children to do the same, and help if necessary.

3 The children take turns doing this, piling up their things in front of them. If they run out of things, they can continue with things they are wearing, parts of their body, and so on (if this is not too much at this stage), but always with things around them. The idea is to see for how long the children can continue before running out of ideas.

At home

Equipment: Class Book page 32.

1 Open Class Books to page 32 and give the children a chance to look at the bottom picture and get a feel for what's happening.

Word set

My things

Equipment: Class Book page 33. "My things" picture cards (see page 133 or Teacher's CD-ROM), vocabulary cards from previous units.

1 Open Class Books to page 33. Appear curious about the page, as if you are trying to figure out what the things are in English. See if the children can tell you. If you ask *What is it?*, ask as if you are not completely sure or ask with a puppet or stuffed animal that genuinely doesn't know.

2 Play any of the games the children know so far using the "My things" picture cards mixed up with other vocabulary cards.

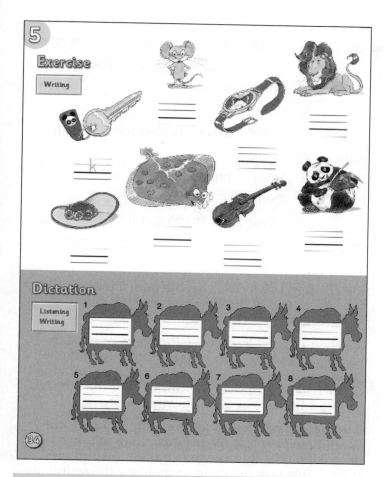

Dictation

Equipment: Class Book page 34. Notebooks. Class Audio (optional).

1 Open Class Books to page 34. Dictate gently or play the recording:

1 wuh- watch
2 muh- mouse
3 fuh- fish
4 guh- gorilla
5 luh- lion
6 huh- hat
7 vuh- violin
8 u- umbrella

Repeat each letter as many times as necessary.

2 If necessary, the children can do more of the same kind of practice in their notebooks.

Exercise

Equipment: Class Book page 34. The alphabet and vocabulary cards learned so far. Notebooks.

1 The children look at pictures on the reverse side of the alphabet cards. They say the associated letters, either individually or as a group.

2 Open Class Books to page 34. Look at the Exercise section as if you are wondering how to do it, and encourage the children to show you.

3 The children write the letters themselves, if possible.

4 Open notebooks. The children write the starting letter of each picture that you or one of the children holds up.

A sample plan for the first lesson

1   Introducing the sounds
2   1–30
3   Phonic mime
4   Introducing the words
5   A game or song from a previous unit
6   Counting sheep
7   Writing the letters
8   Home Book preparation

A sample plan for a follow-up lesson

1   A game or song from a previous unit
2   Game – *Up down*
3   Count
4   A game or song from a previous unit
5   *I have …*
6   Song – *Potato Chant*
7   Exercise
8   Home Book preparation

Phonics

Introducing the sounds

Equipment: Class Book page 35. Yy, Zz, Rr, Xx alphabet cards and the alphabet cards from previous units. Class Audio (optional).

1 Play one of the games from a previous unit using the alphabet cards from the previous units. When the children are focused on the game, innocently slip one or two of the new alphabet cards into the game and step back.

2 When the children notice the cards or need to identify the sound they make in order to play the game, give them a chance to try to guess the sound of the letters, turn over the cards to see the pictures on the other side or ask you what they are.

3 If they do not do any of these things or try but cannot guess one of the sounds, smile mischievously or look puzzled in order to stimulate their interest in solving this new puzzle, and then say the sound of one of the letters with them (e.g., *yuh*). Encourage one of the children to turn over the card. If they cannot say *yacht* by themselves, help them.

4 The children discover each of the sounds in a similar way, and refer to them as *yuh- yacht* or just *yuh, zuh- zebra* or *zuh, ruh- ring* or *ruh,* and *ks- box* or *ks.*

5 Open Class Books to page 35. Appear fascinated by the page. Let the children guess what is happening. If the children don't or can't say the letter on the page, point to the letter **Yy** and indicate the children should do the same. All the children say *yuh- yacht* together. Continue with the other letters.

Option: Play the recording for model pronunciation.

Variation on the first three steps suggested above:
1 Either hold up the **Yy** card, look at it curiously and smile, or hide it behind something (e.g., a book, a toy or your back) and slowly reveal it to the children. If the children are wondering what the letter is and possibly making suggestions but can't or don't say the sound of the letter, say *yuh*. Encourage the children to say this with you. They should feel that they are discovering this with you, not saying it after you.

2 Either show the children the yacht on the other side of the card, encourage one of the children to turn it over, hide the picture and slowly reveal it or gradually draw a picture of a yacht. If the children can't guess what to say, say *yacht* with them. The objective is for them to feel that both they and you are discovering something together.

3 Turn back to the letter **Yy** and encourage the children to practice saying *yuh- yacht* a little.

Phonic mime

1 Mime putting a ring on your finger, and encourage the children to guess the sound you are thinking of. You could give them a hint by suggesting *zuh- zebra?* If they don't say *ruh- ring* themselves, help them say this.

2 See if the children can figure out mimes for **Yy**, **Zz**, and **Xx**. If they need help, do your own mimes for letters they can't think of mimes for, such as sitting on the edge of a yacht to balance it, moving and making the sound of wind blowing for **Yy**, marking stripes on your body with your finger and then galloping for **Zz**, putting things in a box and then folding it closed for **Xx**.

3 These mimes can sometimes be used from now on when the children are saying the sound of a letter, or as hints when the children are trying to spell a word.

Writing the letters

Equipment: Notebooks.

1 Write **Z** on the board, saying the sound and/or miming a zebra as you do so. Then quickly erase it with a playful grin. The children try to write the letter in their notebooks. (If the class is small, they can write on the board with you.)

2 Write **Z** again a bit more slowly, stroke by stroke, and then quickly erase it.

3 Do the same for **z**.

4 Get one of the children to write **Zz** on the board. You can hint by drawing one or both of the letters in the air with your finger. All the children then write **Zz** a few times in their notebooks.

Repeat this procedure for each of the other letters.

Home Book

The Home Book pages can be completed at any point between here and the end of the unit. Before being asked to do any of the exercises in the Home Book, children should be shown exactly what they are expected to do.

Children write the letters as neatly as possible.

Children write the letters as neatly as possible.

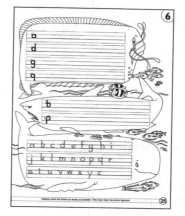

Children write the letters as neatly as possible. They then trace the whole alphabet.

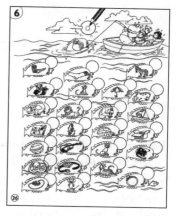

Children write the starting letter next to each picture.

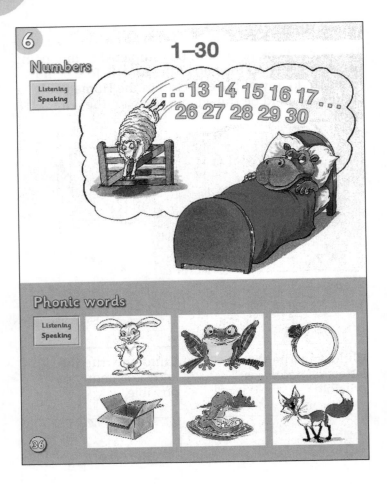

Counting sheep

Equipment: Class Book page 36. Some animal vocabulary cards, including a sheep.

1 Open Class Books to page 36. Appear fascinated by the picture. Let the children guess what is happening.

2 Hold up the picture of a sheep, slowly draw a sheep, or gradually reveal it, and elicit the question and answer *What is it? It's a sheep.*

3 Close your eyes and start counting with the children, *1 sheep, 2 sheep, 3 sheep, 4 sheep … .* As you do so, pretend to fall asleep.

4 Continue for other animals, *1 cow, 2 cows … , 1 horse, 2 horses … .* There is no need to analyze the way the ending changes – the children just enjoy the activity.

5 Put the children into pairs and give them some animal cards. One of them closes her eyes and starts counting, and the other one helps her count. Walk around the class, gently correcting the noun endings where necessary.

> **Teaching tip:** The objective of this activity is to gently introduce the idea that the ending of a noun may change when it is plural. There is no need to analyze. The children will learn more by simply enjoying the activity and by trying and making mistakes.

Numbers

1–30

Equipment: A soft ball and/or a stuffed animal. Class Audio (optional).

1 Say and mime *Please stand up*. Gesture that you are going to throw the ball to one of the children and get the children to say *one* with you.

2 Indicate that the child who has the ball should throw it to somebody else. The whole class says *two*. The children continue counting up to 30. If they find 12–30 difficult, help after giving them a chance to wonder and maybe guess what the next number is.

3 The children do the activity again throwing a stuffed animal or a different kind of ball.

Option: Play the recording.

> **Teaching tip:** Throwing a ball is a useful way to learn and practice many words and patterns. The children can learn sequences such as numbers or days of the week; categories such as vegetables or colors; patterns such as *I like …* or *I can …* ; tell stories with each child adding a sentence; and so on. In fact, there are endless possibilities.

Phonic words

Introducing the words

Equipment: Class Book page 36. Rabbit, frog, ring, box, hippopotamus, fox vocabulary cards and vocabulary cards from previous units. These cards can be supplemented with real objects or toys.

1 Hide one of the new pictures and slowly reveal it or gradually draw a picture of it. If the children don't say *What is it?* with genuine curiosity, continue slowly revealing or drawing the picture, and, if necessary, finally help them say *What is it?*

2 When they ask you the question, pretend you can't hear or tease them a little in another way, in order to get them to ask you again.

3 Discover the answer with them: *It's a (fox).*

4 Get the children to reveal other cards slowly or draw pictures of the things on the cards to stimulate them to ask and answer the question *What is it?* among themselves. Help with either the question or answers when necessary.

5 The children play one of the flashcard games from the previous units with the vocabulary cards from this unit mixed up with the cards from previous units.

6 Open Class Books to page 36. The children ask and answer *What is it? It's a …* about the pictures.

Game

Up down

Equipment: Class Book page 37.

1 Open Class Books to page 37. Appear fascinated by the page. Give the children time to guess what is happening.

2 Close Class Books. Point your finger up and encourage the children to start counting *One, two, three …* . Point your finger down. If the children continue counting … *four, five, six* just smile and say *Uh-oh!* or use a stuffed animal to do this. If necessary, help them start counting back down.

3 Once the children understand the activity, point your finger horizontally. If the children count up or down, smile and either say or use a stuffed animal to say *Uh-oh!* If necessary, help the children repeat the same number until you move your finger up or down.

4 The children do the same activity in pairs or groups.

Variations: This activity can be used for counting in multiples of two, five, ten, and so on. Two fingers can be used to indicate that the speed should double.

The activity can also be used for other language targets by using a pile of cards or words instead of numbers. When one child points her finger up, a child (or group of children) moves the top card face down onto another pile, saying or reading each one. A finger pointing down means the cards need to be moved back again, and a horizontal finger means the card needs to be repeated.

2 Say *I have one (computer)*. Challenge one of the children to say *I have two … ,* The children then continue, *I have three … , I have four … ,* and they see how far they can go. When they run out of ideas, they can start again.

Teaching tip: One of the objectives of this activity is to encourage the children to want to know the English for things they are trying to say. If necessary, give hints (such as giving the starting sound) or help them when they are trying to say new words.

Words in action

Count

Equipment: Class Book page 38. Pictures showing many objects or animals.

1 Open Class Books to page 38 and give the children a chance to look at the top picture and get a feel for what's happening.

2 Put a picture on the table or board. Say the name of an object or animal, and encourage the children to see how many they can find, counting each time – for example, *1 duck, 2 ducks … .*

3 The children do the same activity in pairs or groups.

4 The children do the activity without pictures, saying the names of things around the room. They can either point at the things or go and touch them each time they count one.

I have …

Equipment: Class Book page 38.

1 Open Class Books to page 38 and give the children a chance to look at the bottom picture and get a feel for what's happening.

Action song

Potato chant

Equipment: Class Book page 39. Three potatoes, other objects (e.g., a tomato, a banana, a toy gorilla – each word should contain two or three syllables).

1 Open Class Books to page 39. Appear fascinated by the page. Let the children guess what is happening.

2 Close Class Books. Hold up a potato and look at it curiously to elicit *What is it?* Feed the answer *It's a potato.*

3 Hit the potato with your fist and say with the children *One potato.*

4 Produce another potato – the more dramatically the better – from your pocket or a bag. Hit the first potato and everybody says *One potato*, hit the second potato and everybody says *Two potatoes.* Continue with a third potato.

5 The children sit or stand in a circle around you and put their fists in front of them.

6 Hit each fist in turn, chanting with the children: *One potato, two potatoes, three potatoes, four, five potatoes, six potatoes, seven potatoes, more.* The fist that is hit on *more* is out, and the child puts it behind her back.

7 Just before starting the chant again, produce one of the other objects (e.g., a tomato, a banana, a melon or a toy gorilla). The children chant *One (banana), two (bananas),* and so on. This time one of the children can be the leader and hit the other children's fists.

8 Continue chanting until only one child has a fist in front of her.

Teaching tip: The next time this chant is used, one of the children can be the leader. It is best if the number of children in the circle is varied; so, for example, split the children into groups, play when one child is absent or play sometimes with you and sometimes with a child as the leader.

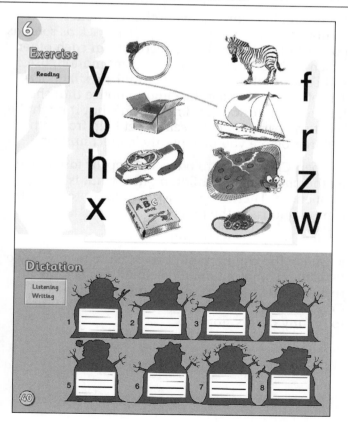

Exercise

Equipment: Class Book page 40. The alphabet, vocabulary and word cards learned so far. Notebooks.

1 The children look at pictures on the reverse side of the alphabet cards. They say the associated letters, either individually or as a group.

2 Open Class Books to page 40. Look at the Exercise section as if you are wondering how to do it, and encourage the children to show you.

3 The children match the letters to the appropriate pictures.

4 Open notebooks. The children write the starting letter of each picture that you hold up. Mix in pictures that have been learned in the Word set sections.

Dictation

Equipment: Class Book page 40. Notebooks. Class Audio (optional).

1 Open Class Books to page 40. Dictate gently or play the recording:

1 ruh- ring
2 luh- lion
3 zuh- zebra
4 puh- panda
5 ks- box
6 guh- gorilla
7 yuh- yacht
8 kwuh- queen

2 Dictate **a**, **d**, **g** and **q** for the children to write in their notebooks so they can see the similarity in the way they are written, without the hand leaving the page.

3 Do the same for **b** and **p** so the children can see that both have two different strokes.

Teaching tip: If the children make mistakes when writing **a, d, g, q, b** and **p**, they may not see the distinction. Dictate these letters occasionally in future lessons, sometimes focusing on them as two different groups of letters, and sometimes mixing them up.

A sample plan for the first lesson

1 Two-letter combinations
2 Game – *Concentration 1*
3 A conversation pattern from a previous unit
4 Varying the vowel
5 Counting sheep
6 A game or song from a previous unit
7 Varying the consonant
8 Home Book preparation

A sample plan for a follow-up lesson

1 Game – *Treasure hunt*
2 Hot – cold
3 A game or song from a previous unit
4 What's cold?
5 Hot/Cold
6 Exercise
7 Dictation
8 Home Book preparation

Phonics

Two-letter combinations

Equipment: Class Book page 41. Two-letter combination cards (see pages 134–137 or Teacher's CD-ROM), alphabet cards from previous units. Class Audio (optional).

1 Play one of the games from a previous unit using the alphabet cards. When the children are focused

on the game, innocently slip some two-letter combinations into the game and step back.

2 When the children notice the cards or need to identify the sound they make in order to play the game, give them a chance to try to guess the sound of the combination cards.

3 If they do not do any of these things or try but cannot guess one of the sounds, smile mischievously or look puzzled in order to stimulate their interest in solving this new puzzle, and then give a hint by hiding the consonant and encouraging them to pronounce the vowel. Then uncover the consonant and encourage them to pronounce the two sounds together, helping if necessary.

4 The children can discover other two-letter combinations in the same way. Step back as soon as possible and let the children learn from each other. When a child mispronounces a combination, use a stuffed animal to say *Uh-oh!* or make a silly noise. The objective is to get the child to notice that she has made a mistake and reflect on what it might be. See if she can correct herself or get help from other children before you give her the correct answer.

5 Open Class Books to page 41. Appear fascinated by the page. Let the children guess what is happening. Then encourage them to try to read the combinations on the page.

Option: Play the recording.

6 Divide the children into two or more teams. Say a two-letter combination. One child from each team rushes to the board to try to write the sound. Continue with a few other combinations, but not too many at this stage.

More two-letter combinations

Variation on the first four steps suggested above:

Equipment: The alphabet cards except c, h, j, q, r, w and y.

1 Hold up the card **Aa**. The children say *a- apple* or just *a*. Hold up the letter **Tt**. The children say *tuh- tiger* or just *tuh*.

2 Move the letters gradually towards each other, with **Tt** to the right of **Aa** as the children look at it. When the cards are touching, look at the children and then the cards curiously, as if to say *How do we say that?* Encourage guessing.

3 Discover the correct pronunciation with the children: *at*. Repeat with them a few times but not too much; otherwise, the spontaneity may be lost. Make sure that the sound of the consonant is unvoiced.

4 Join some other letters together in the same way.

Game

Concentration 1

Equipment: Two-letter combination cards (see pages 134–137 or Teacher's CD-ROM).

1 This game can either be played in groups or as a whole class. The children spread two sets of the two-letter combination cards face down on the table in front of them.

2 The children take turns turning over two cards. If they find a pair of the same sounds, they keep the cards. If the cards are not the same, they turn them face down again, leaving them in the same position. After each card is turned over, the child should read the sound aloud. The winner is the child with the most pairs when all the cards have been claimed.

Teaching tip: If the children mispronounce a combination when playing, such as saying *atuh* instead of *at*, don't drill the correct pronunciation. Draw their attention to the problem, for example by having an animal say *Uh-oh!* or make a silly noise, see if they can correct themselves or do so with help from the other children, and then just get on with the game. It's all natural and fun.

Home Book

The Home Book pages can be completed at any point between here and the end of the unit. Before being asked to do any of the exercises in the Home Book, children should be shown exactly what they are expected to do.

Children write the starting letter under each picture.

Children draw a picture in the frame for each letter, e.g., an apple for **a** and a gorilla for **g**.

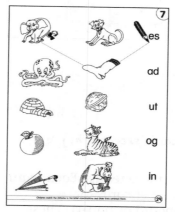

Children match the pictures to the letter combinations and draw lines between them.

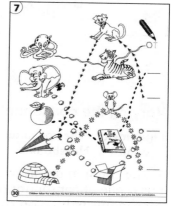

Children follow the trails from the first picture to the second picture to the answer line, and then they write the letter combination.

Combining sounds

Varying the consonant

Equipment: The consonant cards except c, h, j, q, r, w and y. Notebooks.

1 The children are in two or more teams. Each team has a pile of consonant alphabet cards (or consonants written on cardboard or paper). These are on a table or desk at some distance from the board. Write a vowel on the board for each team.

2 The children from each team take turns going to their pile of cards, looking at the top card, putting it at the bottom of the pile, rushing to the board and writing their team's vowel followed by the consonant on the card. The whole team then reads aloud the sound of the combination.

3 Repeat with other vowels.

4 Bring the class together. Write a vowel on the board. Individual children then take turns going to a pile of consonant cards, secretly looking at the top card, and saying the sound made by the vowel followed by the consonant on the card. All the children write the combination in their notebooks.

Varying the vowel

Equipment: Class Book page 42. The alphabet cards except c, h, j, q, r, w and y. Notebooks. Class Audio (optional).

1 The children are in two or more teams. Each team has five vowel cards in a column in front of them. There is also a pile of consonant cards at some distance from where they are.

2 The children from each team take turns going to the pile of cards, taking the top card, rushing back to their group and placing the card to the right of the top vowel. The whole team reads the two-letter combination. The child with the card quickly moves it next to each of the other vowels in turn, with the team reading the combination each time. The next child then rushes to the pile of consonant cards to get the next card.

3 Bring the class together. Write a consonant on the board. Individual children then take turns going to a pile of vowel cards, secretly looking at the top card and saying the sound made by the vowel followed by the consonant on the board. All the children write the combination in their notebooks. Change the consonant on the board and shuffle the vowel cards after all five vowel cards have been used.

4 Open Class Books to page 42. Appear fascinated by the page. Let the children guess what is happening. Then encourage them to try to read the combinations on the page.

Option: Play the recording.

Teaching tip: It is very important for the children to master this stage. It is worth repeating the "Varying the consonant" and "Varying the vowel" activities in future lessons and playing all kinds of games where the children are pronouncing, reading and writing vowel-consonant combinations.

Game

Treasure hunt

Equipment: Class Book page 43. Copies of the treasure map and symbols (see page 138 or Teacher's CD-ROM), 16 two-letter combinations written on cardboard or paper, bag or box.

1 Have a secret copy of the treasure map in front of you. The children should not be able to see the map. Put the symbols for gold, diamonds, sharks and monsters on the map. The sharks can only go in the **sea** squares, but the others can be anywhere.

2 Open Class Books to page 43. Appear fascinated by the page. Let the children guess what is happening. Hand out copies of the treasure maps to each of the children.

Either 3a Put the 16 two-letter combinations into a bag or box. The children take turns drawing combinations from the bag or box and dictating them to the other children. Each child writes each combination on her copy of the map, choosing in which square to write it.

Or 3b Give the children copies of the treasure map with the combinations already written in them. The combinations should be the same for each map, but their location should vary from map to map.

4 The combinations cards are put in a bag or box. Reveal your secret copy of the treasure map to the children. One of the children chooses one of the squares from your map that has a symbol on it, draws out a letter combination card from the bag or box and reads it aloud. If any child has that combination in the square that has been chosen, she gets points for herself or her team.

Teaching tips: The number of cards that are drawn for each symbol square can vary. Between three and five usually works well.

A possible scoring system is:
Gold +10, Diamonds +5, Sharks -3, Monsters -5.

2 Help one child ask *What's hot?, What's cold?, What's very hot?* or *What's very cold?* The other children try to think of as many things as possible. Give hints and help when they are searching for new words.

3 The children do the same for the other three questions.

Words in action

Hot – cold

Equipment: Class Book page 44. Objects or flashcards.

1 Open Class Books to page 44 and give the children a chance to look at the top picture and get a feel for what's happening.

2 One of the children closes her eyes or stands facing the wall while the other children hide an object or flashcard.

3 The child then tries to find the object or card with hints from the other children. When she moves away from it, they should say *Cold!* and when she moves closer they say *Hot!* They can say *Very hot!* when she is very close and *Very cold!* when she is moving far away.

What's cold?

Equipment: Class Book page 44.

1 Open Class Books to page 44 and give the children a chance to look at the bottom picture and get a feel for what's happening.

Word set

Hot / Cold

Equipment: Class Book page 45. "Hot/Cold" picture cards (see page 139 or Teacher's CD-ROM).

1 Open Class Books to page 45. Appear curious about the page as if you are trying to figure out what the things are in English. See if the children can tell you.

2 Give individual children the "Hot/Cold" picture cards. Gesture to a card and the child holding it to indicate that she is the character on the card, and say *How are you?* Encourage her to act out the role – for example, if the answer is *I'm very cold*, encourage her to shiver a lot. The children then ask each other *How are you?* questions.

3 Point to the first picture in the book and make a sentence like *Alaska is very cold*. See if the children can think of some other places that are very cold. The children then do the same for the other pictures. Give hints and help when the children are struggling to express themselves.

> **Teaching tip**: From now on, the children can be encouraged to say things like *I'm hot* or *I'm very cold!* in response to the question *How are you?* or simply when they feel hot or cold.

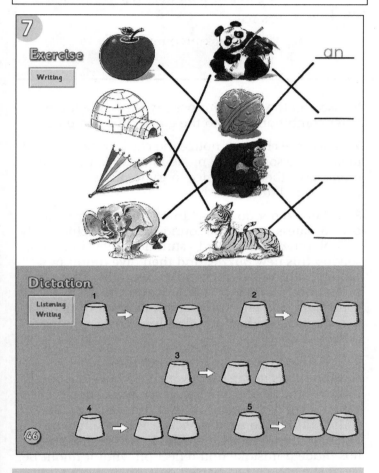

4 Open notebooks. Show the children pairs of pictures. They write two-letter combinations. Place the pairs in a row so that each child can write at her own speed. Do not use vocabulary cards.

Dictation

Equipment: Class Book page 46. Notebooks. Class Audio (optional).

1 Open Class Books to page 46. Dictate gently or play the recording:

1 a- apple, ag
2 e- elephant, ed
3 i- igloo, in
4 o- octopus, ot
5 u- umbrella, ub

2 If necessary, the children can do more of the same kind of practice in their notebooks.

Exercise

Equipment: Class Book page 46. The alphabet cards except c, h, j, q, r, w and y. Notebooks.

1 The children look at the pictures on the reverse side of pairs of alphabet cards. They say the associated sounds, either individually or as a group.

2 Open Class Books to page 46. Look at the Exercise section as if you are wondering how to do it, and encourage the children to show you.

3 The children join the two-letter combinations and write in the appropriate spaces.

A sample plan for the first lesson	A sample plan for a follow-up lesson
1 Three-letter combinations	**1** Game – *Crossword*
2 Game – *Concentration 2*	**2** A conversation pattern from a previous unit
3 A conversation pattern from a previous unit	**3** *Phonic obstacle race*
4 Varying the first consonant	**4** Read and draw
5 "Combining patterns" from a previous unit	**5** Hot–cold
6 A game or song from a previous unit	**6** A game or song from a previous unit
7 Varying the vowel	**7** Exercise
8 Home Book preparation	**8** Home Book preparation

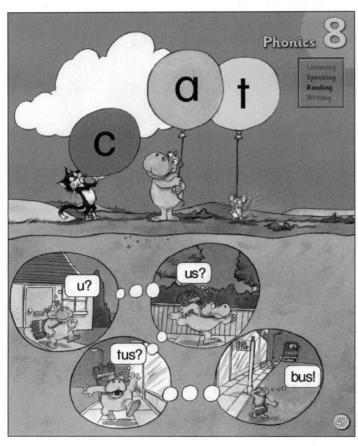

Phonics 8

Listening
Speaking
Reading
Writing

Phonics

Three-letter combinations

Equipment: Class Book page 47. Two-letter combination cards, three-letter combination cards (see pages 134–137 and 140–143 or Teacher's CD-ROM). Class Audio (optional).

1 Play one of the games from a previous unit using two-letter combination cards. When the children are focused on the game, innocently slip some three-letter combinations into the game and step back.

2 When the children notice the cards or need to identify the sound they make in order to play the game, give them a chance to try to guess the sound of the combination cards.

3 If they do not do any of these things or try but cannot guess one of the sounds, smile mischievously or look puzzled in order to stimulate their interest in solving this new puzzle, and then give a hint by hiding both consonants and encouraging them to pronounce the vowel. Then uncover the final consonant and encourage them to pronounce the two sounds together, and finally uncover the first consonant.

4 The children can discover other three-letter combinations in the same way. Step back as soon as possible and let the children learn from each other. When a child mispronounces a combination, use a stuffed animal to say *Uh-oh!* or make a silly noise. The objective is to get the child to notice that she has made a mistake and reflect on what it might be. See if she can correct herself or get help from other children before you give her the correct answer.

5 Open Class Books to page 47. Appear fascinated by the page. Let the children guess what is happening. Then encourage them to try to read the combinations on the page.

Option: Play the recording.

6 Divide the children into two or more teams. Say a three-letter combination. One child from each team rushes to the board to try to write the sound. Continue with a few other combinations, but not too many at this stage.

Three-letter combinations 2

Variation on the first four steps suggested above:

Equipment: The alphabet cards except q.

1 Hold up the card **Aa**. The children say *a- apple* or just *a*. Hold up the letter **Tt**. The children say *tuh- tiger* or just *tuh*.

2 Move the letters gradually toward each other, with **Tt** to the right of the **Aa** as the children look at it. The children read *at*.

3 Move the letter **Cc** towards the other two, on the left of **Aa** as the children look at it. Discover the word *cat* with the children.

4 Join some other letters together in the same way.

> **Teaching tip:** From now on, when the children have difficulty reading or writing a short word, it helps to "build from the vowel." When reading, you or the child covers the consonants before and after the vowel and just reads the vowel. You or the child then uncovers the consonant(s) after the vowel and reads the combination of vowel and consonant(s). Finally, you or the child uncovers the word and reads it. When writing, the same steps can be followed. You (or another child) can dictate the vowel, then the vowel followed by the consonant(s) after the vowel, and finally the whole word.

Game

Concentration 2

Equipment: Three-letter combination cards (see pages 140–143 or Teacher's CD-ROM).

1 This game can either be played in groups or as a whole class. The children spread two sets of the three-letter combination cards face down on the table in front of them.

2 The children take turns turning over two cards. If they find a pair of the same sounds, they keep the cards. If the cards are not the same, they turn them face down again, leaving them in the same position. After each card is turned over, the child should read the sound aloud. The winner is the child with the most pairs when all the cards have been claimed.

> **Teaching tip:** Follow up this game with any of the flashcard games from previous units using three-letter vocabulary cards with the word face up.

Home Book

The Home Book pages can be completed at any point between here and the end of the unit. Before being asked to do any of the exercises in the Home Book, children should be shown exactly what they are expected to do.

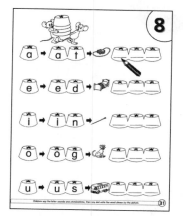

Children say the letter sounds and combinations, and they then say and write the word shown by the picture.

Children read the words. If they find this difficult, have them try to read the middle letter, then the last two letters, then the whole word.

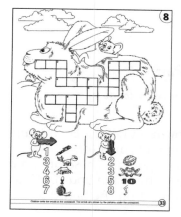

Children write the words in the crossword. The words are shown by the pictures under the crossword.

Children write the words in the spaces under the pictures.

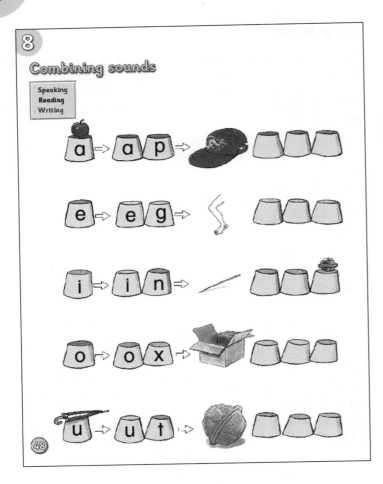

8

Combining sounds

Speaking
Reading
Writing

48

Combining sounds

Varying the first consonant

Equipment: The consonant cards except q. Notebooks.

1 The children are in two or more teams. Each team has a pile of consonant alphabet cards (or consonants written on card or paper). These are on a table or desk at some distance from the board. Write a vowel followed by a consonant on the board for each team.

2 The children from each team take turns going to their pile of cards, looking at the top card, putting it at the bottom of the pile, rushing to the board and writing the consonant from the card followed by their team's vowel-consonant combination. The whole team then reads aloud the three-letter combination.

3 Keep on varying each team's vowel-consonant combination.

4 Bring the class together. Write a vowel-consonant combination on the board. Individual children then take turns going to a pile of consonant cards, secretly looking at the top card, and saying the

sound made by the consonant followed by the vowel-consonant combination on the board. All the children write the combination in their notebooks. While the children are doing this exercise, vary the vowel-consonant combination on the board.

Varying the vowel

Equipment: Class Book page 48. Two piles of alphabet cards, the first with all consonants except q, and the second with all consonants except c, h, j, q, r, w and y. Notebooks. Class Audio (optional).

1 The children are in two or more teams. Each team has five vowel cards in a column in front of them. The two piles of consonant cards are at some distance from where they are and in different parts of the room.

2 One child from each team goes to the first pile of cards, takes the top card, rushes back to her group, and places it to the left of the first vowel. At the same time, another child goes to the second pile, takes the top card, rushes back to her group, and places it to the right of the first vowel. The whole team reads the three-letter combination. The children quickly move the two cards down to the left and right of each of the other vowels in turn, with the team reading the combination each time. The next children then rush to the piles of consonant cards to get the next cards.

3 Bring the class together. Write two consonants on the board with a space between them. Individual children then take turns going to a pile of vowel cards, secretly looking at the top card and saying the sound made when the vowel is put between the two consonants on the board. All the children write the combination in their notebooks. Change the consonants on the board and shuffle the vowel cards after all five vowel cards have been used.

4 Open Class Books to page 48. Appear fascinated by the page. Let the children guess what is happening. Then encourage them to try to read the combinations on the page.

Option: Play the recording.

Teaching tip: It is very important for the children to play around as much as possible with meaningless consonant-vowel-consonant combinations. This will give them the confidence and ability to read and write three-letter words they have never seen before, and it will also prevent them from focusing on memorizing individual words. Playing with "Phonics Builders" (see information on the Teacher's CD-ROM) can be very helpful at this stage.

Game

Crossword

Equipment: Class Book page 49.

1 Open Class Books to page 49. Look at the crossword in your book with a puzzled expression, as if you are wondering what you are supposed to do. Appeal for help from the children.

2 The children try to help you by finding out how the crossword works. This should be a team effort. If they seem to be misunderstanding what they have to do, make tentative suggestions. For example, point to the picture of a cat and to the "1 across" square as if wondering whether there is some connection.

3 Let the children help each other to complete the crossword.

4 Draw another crossword on the board and show picture cards as clues. (The crossword will have to be prepared in advance.)

Teaching tip: From now on, crosswords are frequently used in the Home Book. It is important to make sure that all the children have discovered how they work.

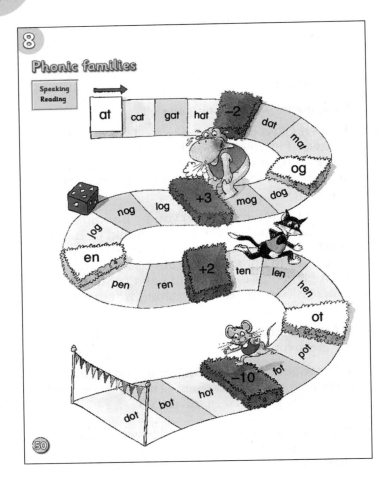

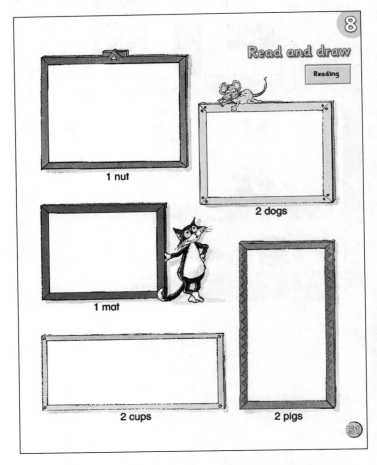

Variations: In a small class, the children can take their moves in turn rather than at the same time. In a larger class, the children can be divided into groups and the children in each group can take their moves in turn.

The copy of the racetrack on the Teacher's CD-ROM can be printed out and enlarged so that a class or group can play together on the same track.

Phonic families

Phonic obstacle race

Equipment: Class Book page 50. Pieces or small toys, die or spinner (see page 129 or Teacher's CD-ROM).

1 Each of the children has a piece or a small toy and a die or spinner. Open Class Books to page 50. Each child places her piece on the **at** square.

2 One child says *Roll!* or *Spin!* and they each roll their die or spin their spinner and move their toy or piece the number of squares indicated on the die or spinner. As they move, they read the sound in each square they pass over or land on. When all the children have finished their move, another child says *Roll!* or *Spin!* and they all roll or spin and move again.

3 If a child lands on a **−2**, **+3**, **+2** or **−10** square, she moves forward or back the number of squares indicated.

4 The game continues until one or all of the children have passed the finishing line.

Read and draw

Equipment: Class Book page 51.

1 Open Class Books to page 51. Look at the page as if you are wondering what to do and encourage the children to show you. If this does not work, pick up a pencil, hesitate as if you are wondering what to draw in the first picture frame, and ask the children for help.

2 If the children don't understand what to do, touch or put your pencil on the word **nut** and look at it curiously as if wondering what it is. If the children can't read it, cover up the **n** and **t** or write **u** on the board. After the children read **u**, add **t** and then **n**, so the children discover *nut*. If necessary, start to draw a nut in the picture frame. Step back and stop giving prompts at whatever stage the children understand what to do.

3 The children read the words and draw the corresponding pictures in each of the other frames.

4 When the children come across a word they haven't seen before, give them a chance to try to read the word. If they can't, build the word from the vowel in the way described in step 2, above. If they can read the word but don't know what it is, mime, gesture or gradually draw a picture to help them guess what it is. For example, pretend to be a pig, or point at or gradually draw a mat.

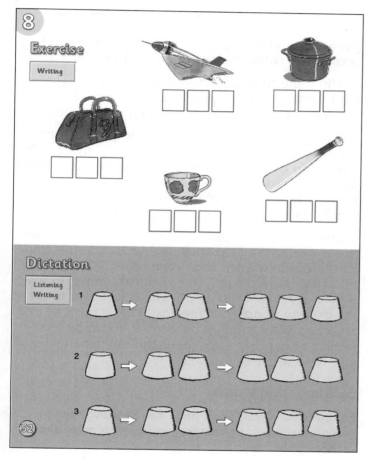

8
Exercise
Writing

Dictation
Listening
Writing

52

Exercise

Equipment: Class Book page 52. Pictures of three-letter word objects. Notebooks.

1 Give one of the children some of the cards that are easiest to spell. She holds up the pictures and all the children spell them in their notebooks. If necessary, help by emphasizing the pronunciation of each letter.

2 If this activity proves much too difficult, switch to something else and come back to it in a later lesson.

If the children seem to be getting the idea, open Class Books to page 52.

3 Look at the Exercise section as if you are wondering what to do. Encourage the children to help you. Focus on the picture of the bag and get them to show you what to do. If they can't figure out what to do, give hints; for example, point to the first box under the picture of the bag with a pencil. Once they have understood what to do, let them continue with the exercise on their own, if possible.

4 Continue by showing more pictures or objects, which the children should try to spell in their notebooks.

Dictation

Three-letter combinations

Equipment: Class Book page 52. Notebooks. Class Audio (optional).

1 Open Class Books to page 52. Dictate gently or play the recording:

> 1 o- octopus – og – pog
> 2 i- igloo – in – min
> 3 u- umbrella – ut – but

The short form of the vowel can be used – for example, *o* instead of *o- octopus*.

2 If necessary, the children can do more of the same kind of practice in their notebooks.

Step-by-step dictation

Equipment: Notebooks.

1 Dictate a vowel and build from the vowel (e.g., *o, ot, mot, hot, pot*). Continue with other vowels.

2 Dictate a three-letter word (or build it from a vowel), and then dictate another word where only the vowel is different (e.g., *pan, pen, pin, pon, pun*). Continue with other consonants.

3 Dictate three-letter combinations (e.g., *pag, tod, but*, and so on).

> **Teaching tip:** If the children find writing difficult, it is worth spending some time on each of the three stages of dictation described above, treating each one as a separate activity. It may be necessary to make writing the main target for a few lessons, switching to supplementary activities and reading games for a change of focus.

A sample plan for the first lesson

1 Reading long words
2 A game or song from a previous unit
3 *How do you spell … ?*
4 Building long words
5 Game – *Concentration 3*
6 "Combining patterns" from a previous unit
7 A game or song from a previous unit
8 Home Book preparation

A sample plan for a follow-up lesson

1 Game – *Letter tiles*
2 Game – *Word race*
3 A conversation pattern from a previous unit
4 *Phonic balloon race*
5 Read and draw
6 Days of the week
7 Exercise
8 Home Book preparation

Phonics 9

Phonics

Reading long words

Equipment: Vocabulary cards

1 Play one of the games from a previous unit with the vocabulary cards. Play the game with the word side of the cards face up, and only include three-letter words. When the children are focused on the game, innocently slip some four-letter (or longer) vocabulary cards into the game and step back.

2 When the children notice the cards or need to read them in order to play the game, give the children a chance to try and read them.

3 If they do not do any of these things or try but cannot read the words, smile mischievously or look puzzled in order to stimulate their interest in solving this new puzzle. Then build their ability to read a word by hiding most of the word and revealing it step by step.

4 The children can discover how to read other words in the same way. Step back as soon as possible and let the children learn from each other. When a child mispronounces a word, use a stuffed animal to say *Uh-oh!* or make a silly noise. The objective is to get the child to notice that she has made a mistake and reflect on what it might be. See if she can correct herself, or get help from other children before you give her the correct answer.

Building long words

Equipment: Class Book page 53. Reading rods or alphabet tiles. Vocabulary cards with more than three letters.

Teaching tip: Reading rods are colorful plastic phonic tiles (see the Teacher's CD-ROM for more information). Alternatively, alphabet tiles made out of plastic or cardboard can be used.

1 Place the five vowel rods or tiles in a column on a table, desk or floor (or write them on the board). The children read each one as you place it.

2 Build words around each vowel using reading rods or alphabet tiles (there is an example in the Class Book). The children read as you place each letter.

3 Open Class Books to page 53. Appear fascinated by the page. Let the children guess what is happening. Then encourage them to try to read the words.

4 Divide the children into two or more teams. Say a long word (real or imaginary). One child from each team rushes to the board to try to write the sound. Continue with other long words.

Teaching tip: It is very important for the children to practice reading words that have no meaning, otherwise the words may be memorized and the children may not internalize the underlying patterns. Reading and writing long meaningless words can be fun, especially if ridiculous sounds or tongue-twisters are used. It can also be effective to include some words in the children's native language, particularly ones that make them laugh.

 Game

Concentration 3

Equipment: All the vocabulary cards learned so far and/or other long words (real or imaginary) written on cards.

1 This game can either be played in groups or as a whole class. The children spread two sets of the cards face down on the table in front of them.

2 The children take turns turning over two cards. If they find a pair of words, they keep the cards. If the cards are not the same, they turn them face down again, leaving them in the same position. After each card is turned over, the child should read the word aloud. The winner is the child with the most pairs when all the cards have been claimed.

Teaching tip: Follow up this game with any of the card games from previous units, using real or imaginary long words.

Home Book

The Home Book pages can be completed at any point between here and the end of the unit. Before being asked to do any of the exercises in the Home Book, children should be shown exactly what they are expected to do.

Children find the words shown by the pictures in the grid. They then match each word to its picture.

Children draw a picture in the space next to each word.

Children write the words in the crossword. The words are shown by the pictures under the crossword.

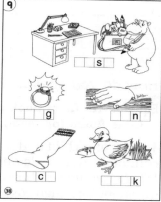

Children write the words in the spaces under the pictures.

Conversation

How do you spell ... ?

Equipment: Class Book page 54. Vocabulary cards. Class Audio (optional).

1 Look at a child and say *How do you spell "cat"?* If she cannot answer, smile and switch to asking children *What's your name?*, *How old are you?* or *How are you?* questions and then casually ask another *How do you spell ... ?* question. Grin as if to say "Here's another puzzle to solve and it's going to be fun."

Either 2a If nobody can answer, point to yourself and get the children to ask you the question. Don't answer until they really want to know. Then either say *cuh- cat, a- apple, tuh- tiger* or *cuh, a, tuh* (use whichever form the class is more used to).

Or 2b If one of the children successfully answers the question, use her answer as the model for the rest of the class.

3 Hold up any vocabulary card, with the picture side facing the children, and say *How do you spell ... ?* The children work on the answer as a group.

4 Divide the class into pairs and give each pair some vocabulary cards. They show one another the pictures and ask and answer the question *How do you spell ... ?*

5 Open Class Books to page 54. Appear fascinated by the page. Let the children guess what is happening.

Option: Play the recording.

Variation: This conversation section can be supplemented with reading rods or letter tiles. One child says *How do you spell ... ?* and another child spells the word with rods or tiles, or other children race to spell the word with rods or tiles. Each child pronounces a letter as she places it.

Game

Letter tiles

Equipment: Class Book page 55. Letter tiles (the vowels and consonants should be different colors) or reading rods – omit c, h, j, q, r, w and y.

1 Open Class Books to page 55. Appear fascinated by the page. Let the children guess what is happening and see if they can read the word on the page.

2 Make a word (with or without meaning) with the rods or tiles and challenge a child to read it. Every alternate letter in the word must be a vowel.

3 Encourage the same child to make a different word and challenge another child to read it. The children can do this in pairs or in circles.

Game

Word race

Equipment: Letter tiles or reading rods for each group – omit c, h, j, q, r, w and y.

1 Divide the class into groups of three to five children. One child in each group is a hippopotamus (Fred).

2 The hippopotamus makes a long word and hides it behind a book or some other kind of screen. She reads the word as many times as is necessary (not letter by letter) and the other children have to try to make the same word with rods or tiles. The first child to complete the word correctly becomes the next hippopotamus. In this game too, every alternate letter must be a vowel.

Game

Long words

Equipment: Letter tiles or reading rods – omit c, h, j, q, r, w and y.

1 One child puts a vowel and consonant pair (e.g., *ap*) on the table, desk or floor.

2 The next child reads it and then adds another vowel and consonant pair (e.g., *apeg*).

3 The game continues in this way, the word getting longer and longer.

Teaching tip: This game can be played in pairs, groups, in a circle or in teams. If there is space and enough tiles or letters, the words can get longer and longer and end up running all around the room.

Game

Guessing letters

Equipment: Pictures of things that have more than three letters, letter tiles or reading rods.

1 Display pictures of a number of things that have the same number of letters (e.g., duck, desk, sock) where all the children can see them. If the board has a ledge, it may be best to place the pictures along it.

2 One of the children secretly chooses one of these words and writes it down on a piece of paper, which the other children cannot see.

3 The other children try to guess which of the words has been chosen by spelling one of the words using rods or tiles. When they have finished, the child who chose the word reveals her piece of paper.

Option: The children (or teams) can get points for guessing correctly.

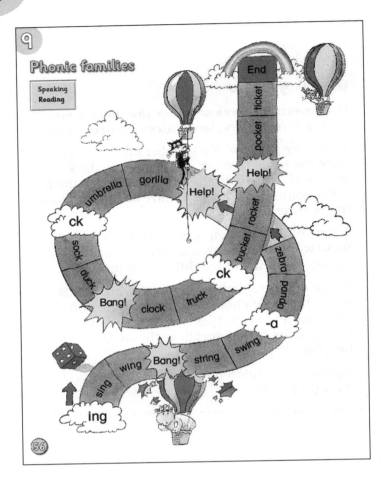

4 The game continues until one or all of the children have passed the finishing line.

Teaching tip: We may need to decide what happens on the special squares the first one or more times the children play these Phonic families games, but, as soon as possible, we can let the children decide.

Variations: In a small class, the children can take their moves in turn rather than at the same time. In a larger class, the children can be divided into groups and the children in each group can take their moves in turn.

The copy of the racetrack on the Teacher's CD-ROM can be printed out and enlarged so that a class or group can play together on the same track.

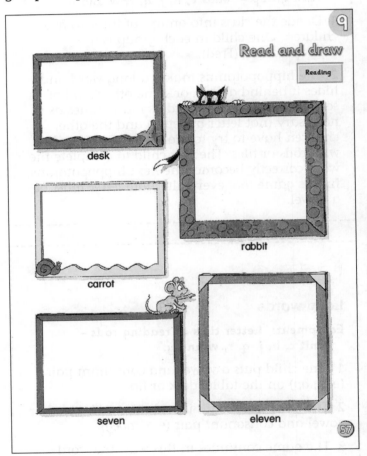

Phonic families

Phonic balloon race

Equipment: Class Book page 56. Pieces or small toys, die or spinner (see page 129 or Teacher's CD-ROM).

1 Each of the children has a piece or a small toy and a die or spinner. Open Class Books to page 56. Each child places her piece on the **ing** square.

2 One child says *Roll!* or *Spin!* and they each roll their die or spin their spinner and move their toy or piece the number of squares indicated on the die or spinner. As they move, they read the sound in each square they pass over or land on. When all the children have finished their move, another child says *Roll!* or *Spin!* and they all roll or spin and move again.

3 If a child lands on the special **Bang!** or **Help!** squares, various things could happen. They could miss one or more turns, have to roll certain numbers in order to move again, move back a certain number of squares, have to count backwards from 20 to 1 or perform some other fun language activity, have to hit a target on the board with a ball, and so on.

Read and draw

Equipment: Class Book page 57.

1 Open Class Books to page 57. Look at the page as if you are wondering what to do and encourage the children to show you.

2 The children read the words and draw the corresponding pictures in each of the frames. If they can't read a word, cover it up except for one of the vowels, and build their ability to read the word by gradually revealing the other letters.

3 When the children come across a word they haven't seen before, give them a chance to try to read the word. If they can't, build the word from the vowel in the way described in step 2, above. If they can read the word but don't know what it is, mime, gesture or gradually draw a picture to help them guess what it is.

they can write the correct letters in the boxes below the pictures. If they can't do this, dictate the words, gradually emphasizing the pronunciation of the missing letters more and more until they can do the exercise.

3 If necessary, continue by showing more pictures or objects, which the children should try to spell in their notebooks.

Teaching tip: If the children have trouble distinguishing *l* and *r*, do not overcorrect them. There is no point in expecting perfection at this stage. It is enough for them to realize that there is a difference between the two letters and for their pronunciation to gradually improve.

Dictation

Long words

Equipment: Class Book page 58. Notebooks. Class Audio (optional).

1 Open Class Books to page 58. Dictate gently or play the recording:

  1 abepigodut
  2 imonusefag

Pause very slightly after each consonant.

2 If necessary, the children can do more of the same kind of practice in their notebooks.

Step-by-step dictation

Equipment: Notebooks.

1 Think of a word that has more than three letters and which the children have already learned (e.g., *lemon*). Dictate one of the vowels in the word (e.g., *e*). Dictate the rest of the word in stages (e.g., *em, lem, lemon*). The children write each stage separately so that each step is clear. If the children seem to be spelling words from memory rather than thinking things through, it is best to switch to words that have no meaning.

2 Dictate whole words, both with and without meanings. If a child finds a word difficult, break it down into its component parts, focusing on a vowel and building the spelling.

Exercise

Equipment: Class Book page 58. Two large pieces of paper. Notebooks.

1 The children draw animals on two pieces of paper and draw a large **l** in one animal and a large **r** in the other. They then play the *a* and *an* game, but instead of *a* and *an* use **l** and **r**.

Option: Instead of touching pictures of animals, the children can growl like dogs, saying *rrr, rrr* when shown a picture that contains an **r** and sing *la, la, la* when shown a picture that contains an **l**.

2 Open Class Books to page 58. Let the children show you what to do in the Exercise section. See if

A sample plan for the first lesson

1 *It's a …*
2 *I don't know*
3 Long words
4 Stretch
5 Game – *Animals*
6 A game or song from a previous unit (with word cards)
7 *Guessing letters*
8 Home Book preparation

A sample plan for a follow-up lesson

1 A game or song from a previous unit
2 Throw
3 A game or song from a previous unit
4 Starting letter
5 Song – *I am Maria*
6 Exercise
7 Dictation
8 Home Book preparation

and answer *What is it? It's a …* as they have done in "Introducing the words" activities in previous units.

2 Open Class Books to page 59 and see if the children can figure out what is written in the speech bubbles.

3 One child points to an animal or object in the picture and asks *What is it?* Another child or other children answer *It's a … .* This can be done in pairs, groups or as a class, with the children taking turns asking the question.

4 Close Class Books. Write the question *What is it?* on the board and encourage the children to figure out what you have written and read the question aloud.

5 Half-draw a picture on the board. Each of the children writes in her notebook what she thinks the picture is using the pattern *It's a … .* Help by dictating *It's a …* if necessary.

6 The children take turns half-drawing pictures and another child or each of the other children writes an *It's a …* sentence in her notebook. This activity can be done in pairs, groups or as a class.

Target pattern

It's a …

Equipment: Class Book page 59. Vocabulary cards. Notebooks.

1 Play one of the games from a previous unit with the vocabulary cards, with either the picture side or the word side of the cards face up. The children ask

Home Book

The Home Book pages can be completed at any point between here and the end of the unit. Before being asked to do any of the exercises in the Home Book, children should be shown exactly what they are expected to do.

Children connect the dots and then complete the question and answer about each picture.

Children draw a picture in the space next to each word.

Children write the words in the crossword. The words are shown by the pictures under the crossword.

Children connect the dots and then write *What is it? It's a …* about each picture in their notebooks.

5 Open Class Books to page 60. Let the children guess what is happening.

Option: Play the recording.

Conversation

I don't know

Equipment: Class Book page 60. Vocabulary cards. Class Audio (optional).

1 Ask a child a question like *What's a sofiapatopolos?*, saying the long word quickly and with a grin. The objective is to get the child to react with a *huh?* or *uh?* or equivalent in their own language. Ask the same or a similar question to one or two other children.

2 Half-draw a meaningless picture a bit flamboyantly on the board, grin and say *What is it?* Draw a bit more of the picture and ask *What is it?* again. When they are looking puzzled, encourage them to ask you *What is it?* Shrug your shoulders and say *I don't know*.

3 Go back to asking one or two children questions like *What's a sofiapatopolos?* If they don't answer *I don't know*, hint by shrugging your shoulders, and, if necessary, say part of the sentence with them.

4 The children do the same in pairs, saying long meaningless words as quickly as possible.

Game

Animals

Equipment: Class Book page 61. Grids (two for each child) and animals (see page 144 or Teacher's CD-ROM).

1 Give two grids, one hippopotamus, one octopus, one frog and three ants to each of the children. Open Class Books to page 61. Appear fascinated by the page. Let the children guess what is happening.

2 Divide the children into pairs. Place a screen between each pair of children, or have them turn back to back.

3 Each child places her animals wherever she likes on one of the grids in front of her.

4 The children take turns trying to guess where the other child's animals are. For example, one child says *Twenty-one. What is it?* The other child may say *It's a frog* or *Nothing* if the square is blank.

5 If the child guesses successfully, she continues choosing squares until the answer is *Nothing*. She marks where the other child's animals are located on her second grid.

6 The winner is the first child to find all the other child's animals. She must successfully locate all the squares that each animal is in. (The hippopotamus is in six squares, the octopus is in five squares, the frog is in three squares and each of the ants is in one square.)

Words in action

Throw

**Equipment: Class Book page 62.
A ball or stuffed animal.**

1 Open Class Books to page 62 and give the children a chance to look at the top picture and get a feel for what's happening.

2 Smile and say *I like (apples)*. Gesture to one of the children and help her say *I like …* . If she cannot finish the sentence, gesture to another child. If necessary, give more examples of things you like such as *I like soccer, I like dogs*, and so on, looking and sounding as if you really like each thing you mention. Then gesture to a child to say what she likes. Only one or two children need to make sentences before moving on to step 3.

3 Say *I like (cats)*. Throw the ball or stuffed animal to one of the children, who makes an *I like …* sentence and throws the ball or stuffed animal to another child, who does the same. Do this for a short time before moving on to step 4.

4 Say *I like (basketball)*. Throw the ball or stuffed animal to one of the children. After she says *I like …* , say *And?*, gesturing for her to say another thing she likes. The next child says three things she likes, the next child four things, and so on. If this activity is too difficult for the children, it may help for them to play in teams, with the other members of the team helping the child who is making the sentences.

Starting letter

Equipment: Class Book page 62.

1 Open Class Books to page 62 and give the children a chance to look at the bottom picture and get a feel for what's happening.

2 Say *I like (d)*, smile and gesture for the children to solve the puzzle. Encourage the children to guess what you like that begins with **d**.

3 The children take turns thinking of other things they like and saying the starting letter, e.g., *I like (h)*.

Action song

I am Maria

Equipment: Class Book page 63. Class Audio.

1 Open Class Books to page 63 and give the children a chance to look at the picture and get a feel for what's happening.

2 Close Class Books. Play the recording.

3 Sing the song with true or absurd (e.g., *I have a gorilla*) sentences about yourself.

4 Encourage individual children to sing the song with true or absurd sentences about themselves, and encourage them to mime or gesture while singing:
With *I am …* , they could point to themselves.
With *I have …* and *I like …* , they could mime the animal or thing they have or like.
With *See you soon*, they could wave goodbye.

Variation: The song can be sung as a round. The second child starts singing *I am …* when the first child sings *I have …* , and the third child starts singing *I am …* when the second child starts singing *I have …* , and so on. After each child finishes the song, she sings it again a certain number of times.

Teaching tip: If the children like the song, it can be used again later in the course with other patterns such as *I can …* , *I live in …* , *I'm from …* , *I hate …* , *I get up at …* , and so on.

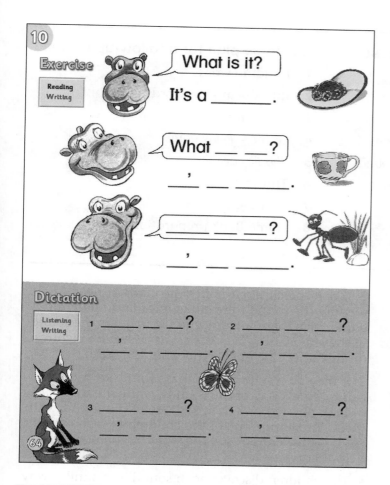

Dictation

**Equipment: Class Book page 64. Notebooks.
Class Audio (optional).**

1 Open Class Books to page 64. Dictate gently or play the recording:

1 What is it? It's a cat.
2 What is it? It's a dog.
3 What is it? It's a bag.
4 What is it? It's a pot.

2 If necessary, the children can do more of the same kind of practice in their notebooks.

Exercise

**Equipment: Class Book page 64. Vocabulary cards.
Notebooks.**

1 Open Class Books to page 64. Look at the Exercise section as if you are wondering what to do. Encourage the children to help you. Focus on the first line and have them teach you to read *What is it?*

2 The children write the questions and answers in the Class Book.

3 Open notebooks. Place some vocabulary cards in a row, with the pictures facing the children. The ledge along the bottom of a board is a convenient place. The children write a question and answer for each card. If the children have difficulty writing a word, dictate it step by step, building from a vowel.

Teaching tip: From now on, writing sentences about picture cards becomes one of the most important ways of practicing writing.

A sample plan for the first lesson

1 Introducing the sounds
2 At home
3 Phonic mime
4 A game or song from a previous unit
5 Game – *Playing with phonic sounds*
6 "Combining patterns" from a previous unit
7 Game – *Writing the sounds*
8 Home Book preparation

A sample plan for a follow-up lesson

1 Building words
2 Introducing the words
3 Counting sheep
4 Game – *Relay game*
5 *Phonic car race*
6 Throw
7 Exercise
8 Home Book preparation

Phonics

Introducing the sounds

Equipment: Class Book page 65. ee, ea, ch and sh double-letter cards (see page 145 or Teacher's CD-ROM) and the alphabet cards from previous units. Class Audio (optional).

1 Play one of the games from a previous unit using the alphabet cards from the previous units. When the children are focused on the game, innocently slip one or two of the new double-letter cards into the game and step back.

2 When the children notice the cards or need to identify the sound they make in order to play the game, give them a chance to try to guess the sound of the letters, turn over the cards to see the pictures on the other side or ask you what they are.

3 If they do not do any of these things or try but cannot guess one of the sounds, smile mischievously or look puzzled and then say one of the sounds with them. Encourage one of the children to turn over the card. If they cannot say the word by themselves, help them.

4 The children discover each sound in a similar way and refer to them as *ee- tree* or just *ee*, *ea- seal* or *ea*, *chuh- chicken* or *chuh* and *shuh- ship* or *shuh*.

5 Open Class Books to page 65. Appear fascinated by the page. Let the children guess what is happening. If the children don't or can't say the sounds on the page, point to the letters **ee** and indicate that the children should do the same. Say *ee- tree* together. Continue with the other sounds.

Option: Play the recording for model pronunciation.

Variation on the first three steps suggested above:
1 Either hold up the **ee** card, look at it curiously and smile, or hide it behind something (e.g., a book, a toy or your back) and slowly reveal it to the children. If the children are wondering what the sound is and possibly making suggestions but can't or don't say the sound, say *ee*. Encourage the children to say this with you. They should feel that they are discovering this with you.

2 Either show the children the tree on the other side of the card, encourage one of the children to turn it over, hide the picture and slowly reveal it, or gradually draw a picture of a tree. If the children can't guess what to say, say *tree* with them.

3 Turn back to the **ee** and encourage the children to practice saying *ee- tree* a little.

Phonic mime

1 Mime being a tree with your branches spread out and encourage the children to guess the sound you are thinking of. You could give them a hint by suggesting *sh- ship*? If they don't say *ee- tree* themselves, help them say this.

2 See if the children can figure out mimes for *ea, ch* and *sh*. If they need help, do your own mimes for sounds they can't think of mimes for, such as clapping your hands like a circus seal for *ea*, walking and moving your neck forwards and backwards for *ch*, and miming waves with your hand and then joining your hands in a point to indicate a bow moving through the waves for *sh*.

3 These mimes can sometimes be used from now on when the children are saying the phonic sounds, or as hints when the children are trying to spell a word.

Game

Playing with phonic sounds

Equipment: Letter tiles or reading rods and tiles or rods for this unit's double-letter sounds (the vowels and consonants should be different colors, and the double-letter sounds can be either be the same color as the vowels or a third color).

1 One child makes a long word with rods or tiles and hides it behind a book or screen.

2 She reads the word as many times as is necessary (not letter by letter) and the other children have to try to make the same word with rods or tiles.

3 The first child to complete the word correctly makes the next word.

Variation:

1 One child puts a vowel or double-letter sound and consonant pair (e.g., *ap* or *eep*) made with rods or tiles on the table, desk or floor.

2 The next child reads it and then adds another vowel or double-letter sound and consonant pair (e.g., *apeg* or *eepeg*).

3 The game continues in this way, the word getting longer and longer.

Teaching tip: In both activities it is easiest to alternate vowels and double-letter sounds.

Home Book

The Home Book pages can be completed at any point between here and the end of the unit. Before being asked to do any of the exercises in the Home Book, children should be shown exactly what they are expected to do.

Children practice writing the letter combinations and then figure out how to spell the words below.

Children practice writing the letter combinations and then figure out how to spell the words below.

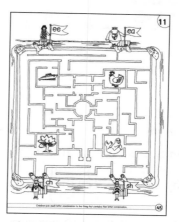

Children match each letter combination to the thing that contains that letter combination.

Children match the dots and then complete the question and answer about each picture.

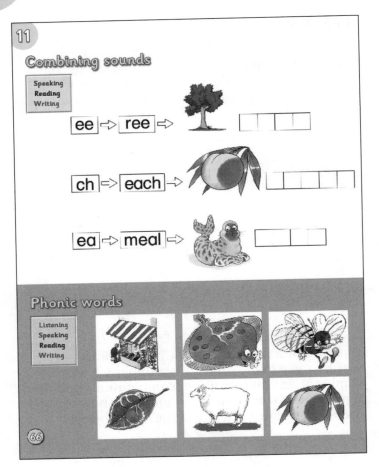

Combining sounds

Phonic words

Introducing the words

Equipment: Class Book page 66. Shop, fish, bee, leaf, sheep, peach vocabulary cards and vocabulary cards from previous units. These cards can be supplemented with real objects or toys.

1 Play one of the games from a previous unit using the new vocabulary cards mixed in with vocabulary cards from previous units. The cards should have their written side face up.

2 When the children notice the new cards or need to read them in order to play the game, give them a chance to try to guess how to read the word. If they can't do so, they could turn the card over to find out what the word is. Give hints if necessary.

3 Open Class Books to page 66. The children ask and answer *What is it? It's a …* about the pictures.

Variation: The children can do an activity that involves writing. For example, one child can show a picture of one of the new or old vocabulary cards and the other children or one child from each team can race to the board to spell it.

Game

Writing the sounds

1 This activity can be done as a whole class or in teams. Say *ee* and the children (or one child from each team) race to the board to write the sound.

2 Do the same for other sounds and individual letters or get one of the children to say the sounds or letters.

Combining sounds

Building words

Equipment: Class Book page 66.

1 Start with *Writing the sounds*, above, and mix in or lead on to real or imaginary words. For example, you could say *ee* followed by *lee*, then *leep* and then *sleep*.

2 Open Class Books to page 66. All point to **ee**. One of the children or the whole class reads the sound. Do the same for **ree**. The children try to write *tree* in their books.

3 The children try to figure out the spelling of the other words.

Variation: Dictate similar sequences for the children to write in their notebooks. For example, say *ea*, then *each* and then *teach*.

Game

Relay game

Equipment: Class Book page 67. The vocabulary cards from this unit and some from previous units.

1 Open Class Books to page 67. Appear fascinated by the page. Let the children guess what is happening.

2 Divide the children into teams. It is usually best to only have two teams unless the board is very large.

3 Each team forms a line leading away from the board. The front child on each team should be the same distance from the board.

4 Hold up a card with the picture side facing the children. The first child on each team races to the board and tries to spell the word on the board. The other members of each team help by saying letters, for example, *a- apple* or just *a* (as in *apple*). Later in the game, a child can hold up the card.

5 When a child finishes spelling the word, she runs back to her team, touches the next child and goes to the back of the line.

6 Hold up another card for the next child on each team to spell. Each team will go at a different speed, so put the previous cards in a place where all the children can see them (e.g., along the board ledge).

7 The game ends when all the children on one team have spelled a word. If there are few children in the class, it is possible to decide in advance that each child should spell two or three words.

Phonic families

Phonic car race

Equipment: Class Book page 68. Pieces or small toys, die or spinner (see page 129 or Teacher's CD-ROM).

1 Each of the children has a piece or small toy and a die or spinner. Open Class Books to page 68. Each child places her piece on the **ee** square.

2 One child says *Roll!* or *Spin!* and they each roll their die or spin their spinner and move their toy or piece the number of squares indicated on the die or spinner. As they move, they read the sound in each square they pass over or land on. When all the children have finished their move, another child says *Roll!* or *Spin!* and they all roll or spin and move again.

3 If a child lands on the special **Screech!** or **Crash!** squares, various things could happen: they could miss one or more turns, have to roll certain numbers in order to move again, move back a certain number of squares, have to count backwards from 20 to 1 or perform some other fun language activity, have to hit a target on the board with a ball, and so on.

4 The game continues until one or all of the children have passed the finishing line.

Variations: In a small class, the children can take their moves in turn rather than at the same time. In a larger class, the children can be divided into groups and the children in each group can take their moves in turn.

The copy of the racetrack on the Teacher's CD-ROM can be printed out and enlarged so that a class or group can play together on the same track.

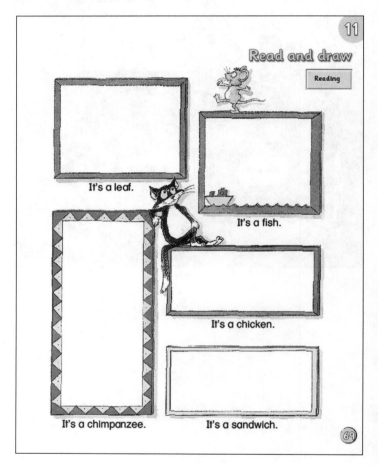

Read and draw

Equipment: Class Book page 69.

1 Open Class Books to page 69. Look at the page as if you are wondering what to do and encourage the children to show you.

2 The children read the words and draw the corresponding pictures in each of the frames. If they can't read a word, cover it up except for one of the vowels or double-letter sounds, and build their ability to read the word by gradually revealing the other letters.

3 When the children come across a word they haven't seen before, give them a chance to try to read the word. If they can't, build the word from the vowel in the way described in step 2, above. If they can read the word but don't know what it is, mime, gesture or gradually draw a picture to help them guess what it is.

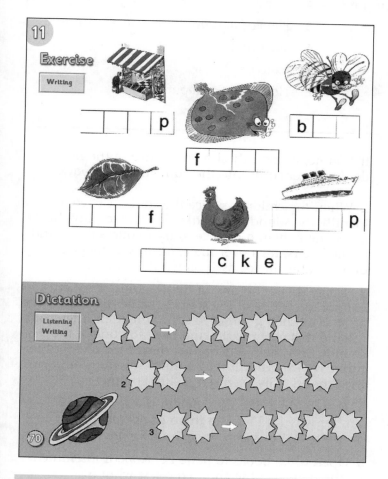

Equipment: Class Book page 70. Notebooks. Class Audio (optional).

1 Open Class Books to page 70. Dictate gently or play the recording:

   1 ch- chicken – chop
   2 ee- tree – chee
   3 sh- ship – shed

2 Dictate one of the double-letter sounds from this unit and build from the sounds (e.g., *ee- tree, eep, seep, meep, meet*).

3 Dictate a word (or build it from a vowel), and then dictate another word where the vowel or double-letter sound has been changed (e.g., *sot, set, seet, sheet*).

Exercise

Equipment: Class Book page 70. Vocabulary cards. Notebooks.

1 Open Class Books to page 70. Each of the children tries to write the words in the spaces below each picture. After they have tried their best, give hints to help them complete the words.

2 Place vocabulary cards with the picture side facing the children – perhaps along the board ledge. The children write the question and answer *What is it? It's a …* about each picture. Each child goes at her own speed.

A sample plan for the first lesson

1 Introducing the sounds
2 Touch
3 Phonic mime
4 A game or song from a previous unit
5 Playing with phonic sounds
6 "Combining patterns" from a previous unit
7 Writing the sounds
8 Home Book preparation

A sample plan for a follow-up lesson

1 Building words
2 Introducing the words
3 Count
4 Game – *Alien game*
5 *Phonic jungle race*
6 Starting letter
7 Exercise
8 Home Book preparation

Phonics 12

Listening
Speaking
Reading
Writing

Phonics

Introducing the sounds

Equipment: Class Book page 71. oo, o̅o̅, ar and ou double-letter cards (see page 146 or Teacher's CD-ROM), the double-letter cards on page 145 and the alphabet cards from previous units. Class Audio (optional).

1 Play one of the games from a previous unit using the alphabet and double-letter cards from the previous units. When the children are focused on

the game, innocently slip one or two of the new double-letter cards into the game and step back.

2 When the children notice the cards or need to identify the sound they make in order to play the game, give them a chance to try to guess the sound of the letters, turn over the cards to see the pictures on the other side or ask you what they are.

3 If they do not do any of these things or try but cannot guess one of the sounds, smile mischievously or look puzzled in order to stimulate their interest in solving this new puzzle, and then say one of the sounds with them. Encourage one of the children to turn over the card. If they cannot say the word on the other side by themselves, help them.

4 The children discover each of the sounds in a similar way and refer to them as *oo- foot* or just *oo*, *ar- car* or *ar*, *o̅o̅- spoon* or *o̅o̅*, and *ou- house* or *ou*.

5 Open Class Books to page 71. Appear fascinated by the page. Let the children guess what is happening. If the children don't or can't say the sounds on the page, point to the letters **oo** and indicate that the children should do the same. All the children say *oo- foot* together. Continue with the other sounds.

Option: Play the recording for model pronunciation.

Variation on the first three steps suggested above:
1 Either hold up the **oo** card, look at it curiously and smile, or hide it behind something (e.g., a book, a toy or your back) and slowly reveal it to the children. If the children are wondering what the sound is and possibly making suggestions but can't or don't say the sound, say *oo*. Encourage the children to say this with you. They should feel that they are discovering this with you, not saying it after you.

2 Either show the children the foot on the other side of the card, encourage one of the children to turn it

over, hide the picture and slowly reveal it or gradually draw a picture of a foot. If the children can't guess what to say, say *foot* with them. The objective is for them to feel that both they and you are discovering something together.

3 Turn back to the **oo** and encourage the children to practice saying *oo- foot* a little.

Phonic mime

1 Mime driving a car, and encourage the children to guess the sound you are thinking of. You could give them a hint by suggesting *ou- house?* If they don't say *ar- car* themselves, help them say this.

2 See if the children can figure out mimes for **oo**, **o͞o** and **ou**. If they need help, do your own mimes for sounds they can't think of mimes for, such as holding up your foot and pointing to it for **oo**, eating with a spoon for **o͞o**, and putting your hands above your head in the shape of a roof for **ou**.

3 These mimes can sometimes be used from now on when the children are saying the phonic sounds, or as hints when the children are trying to spell a word.

Playing with phonic sounds

Equipment: Letter tiles or reading rods and tiles or rods for the double-letter sounds learned so far (the vowels and consonants should be different colors, and the double-letter sounds can be either the same color as the vowels or a third color).

1 One child makes a long word with rods or tiles and hides it behind a book or some other kind of screen.

2 She reads the word as many times as is necessary (not letter by letter), and the other children have to try to make the same word with rods or tiles.

3 The first child to complete the word correctly makes the next word.

Variation:
1 One child puts a vowel or double-letter sound and consonant pair (e.g., *ap* or *eep*) made with rods or tiles on the table, desk or floor.

2 The next child reads it and then adds another vowel or double-letter sound and consonant pair (e.g., *apeg* or *eepeg*).

3 The game continues in this way, the word getting longer and longer.

Teaching tip: In both activities it is easiest if alternate tiles or rods are a vowel or a double-letter sound.

Writing the sounds

1 This activity can be done as a whole class or in teams. Say *oo* and the children (or one child from each team) race to the board to write the sound.

2 Do the same for other sounds and individual letters, or get one of the children to say the sounds or letters.

Home Book

The Home Book pages can be completed at any point between here and the end of the unit. Before being asked to do any of the exercises in the Home Book, children should be shown exactly what they are expected to do.

Children practice writing the letter combinations and then figure out how to spell the words below.

Children practice writing the letter combinations and then figure out how to spell the words below.

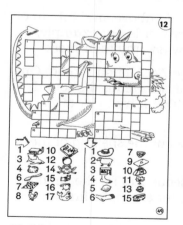

Children write the words in the crossword. The words are shown by the pictures under the crossword.

Children connect the dots and then write *What is it? It's a ...* about each picture.

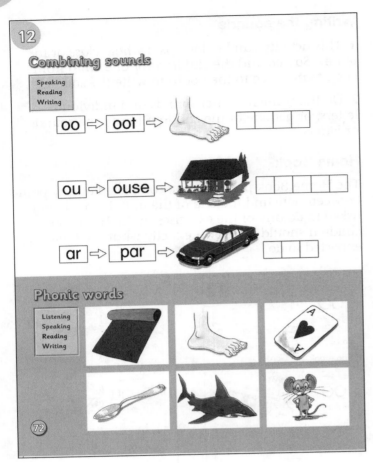

Combining sounds

Building words

Equipment: Class Book page 72.

1 Start with *Writing the sounds*, above, and mix in or lead on to real or imaginary words. For example, you could say *ar* followed by *ark* and then *shark*.

2 Open Class Books to page 72. All point to **oo**. One of the children or the whole class reads the sound. Do the same for *oot*. The children try to write *foot* in their books.

3 The children try to figure out the spelling of the other words.

Variation: Dictate similar sequences for the children to write in their notebooks, for example, first *oo*, then *ook*, then *book*.

Phonic words

Introducing the words

Equipment: Class Book page 72. Carpet, book, card, igloo, shark, mouse vocabulary cards and vocabulary cards from previous units. These cards can be supplemented with real objects or toys.

1 Play one of the games from a previous unit using the new vocabulary cards mixed in with vocabulary cards from previous units. The cards should have their written side face up.

2 When the children notice the new cards or need to read them in order to play the game, give them a chance to try to guess how to read the word. If they can't do so, they could turn the card over to find out what the word is. Give hints if necessary.

3 Open Class Books to page 72. The children ask and answer *What is it? It's a ...* about the pictures.

Variation: The children can do an activity that involves writing. For example, one child can show a picture of one of the new or old vocabulary cards and the other children or one child from each team can race to the board to spell it.

Game

Alien game

Equipment: Class Book page 73. The vocabulary cards from this unit and from previous units.

1 Open Class Books to page 73. Appear fascinated by the page. Let the children guess what is happening.

2 Close Class Books. One child (or the teacher) is the hippopotamus and stands in front of the class with the vocabulary cards. She secretly chooses one of the cards (e.g., shirt), looks at the written side, notices how many letters there are in the word and draws the same number of dashes (e.g., _ _ _ _ _) on the board.

3 The other children take turns, either individually or as team members, guessing the spelling of the word. Each child says a letter (e.g., *suh- sock*).

4 If the word contains the letter, the hippopotamus writes the letter in the appropriate space or spaces. If the word does not contain the letter, the hippopotamus draws one part of the alien on the board.

5 The objective of the game is to spell the word before the alien is completely drawn.

Game

Home

Equipment: One or more copies of the game board (see page 147 or Teacher's CD-ROM), pieces, die or number cards.

1 Either write a double-letter sound in the space in one of the corners of the game board or dictate it for the children to write. Then choose words (with or without a meaning) that include that double-letter sound and write or dictate one in each of the spaces on the ladder leading from that corner. Do the same for the other three corners and ladders.

2 Each child places a piece in one of the corners, and the children take turns rolling the die or choosing a number card and moving their pieces toward **Home**. When a child moves her piece onto a word, she reads the word.

3 A child must get exactly the right number to land on **Home**. If the number is too large, she must continue moving her piece down one of the other ladders on the other side of **Home** and try to move toward **Home** again on the next turn.

Teaching tip: In a small class, there can be just one game board. In a larger class, there can be one board for each group.

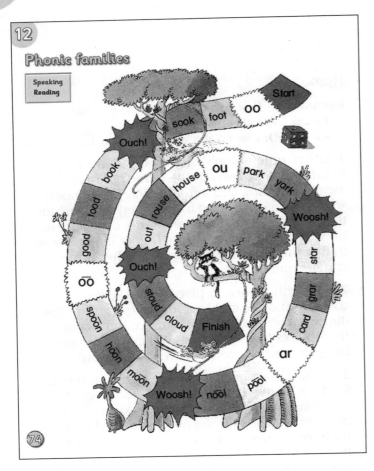

Phonic families

Speaking
Reading

language activity, have to hit a target on the board with a ball, and so on.

4 The game continues until one or all of the children have passed the finishing line.

Variations: In a small class, the children can take their moves in turn rather than at the same time. In a larger class, the children can be divided into groups and the children in each group can take their moves in turn.

The copy of the racetrack on the Teacher's CD-ROM can be printed out and enlarged so that a class or group can play together on the same track.

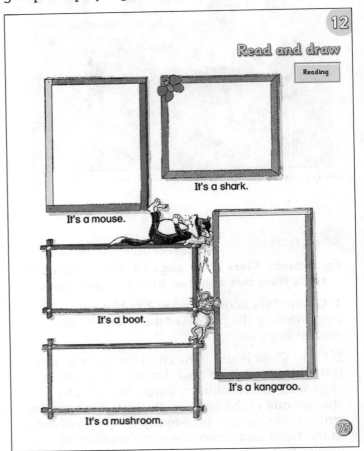

Phonic families

Phonic jungle race

Equipment: Class Book page 74. Pieces or small toys, die or spinner (see page 129 or Teacher's CD-ROM).

1 Each of the children has a piece or small toy and a die or spinner. Open Class Books to page 74. Each child places her piece on the **Start** square.

2 One child says *Roll!* or *Spin!* and they each roll their die or spin their spinner and move their toy or piece the number of squares indicated on the die or spinner. As they move, they read the sound in each square they pass over or land on. When all the children have finished their move, another child says *Roll!* or *Spin!* and they all roll or spin and move again.

3 If a child lands on the special **Ouch!** or **Woosh!** squares, various things could happen: they could miss one or more turns, have an extra turn, have to roll certain numbers in order to move again, move back a certain number of squares, have to count backwards from 20 to 1 or perform some other fun

Read and draw

Equipment: Class Book page 75.

1 Open Class Books to page 75. Look at the page as if you are wondering what to do and encourage the children to show you.

2 The children read the words and draw the corresponding pictures in each of the frames. If they can't read a word, cover it up except for one of the vowels or double-letter sounds, and build their ability to read the word by gradually revealing the other letters.

3 When the children come across a word they haven't seen before, give them a chance to try to read the word. If they can't, build the word from the vowel in the way described in step 2, above. If they can read the word but don't know what it is, mime, gesture or gradually draw a picture to help them guess what it is.

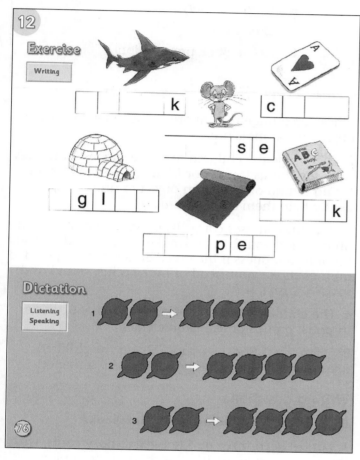

Dictation

Equipment: Class Book page 76. Notebooks. Class Audio (optional).

1 Open Class Books to page 76. Dictate gently or play the recording:

   1 ar- car – par
   2 $\overline{oo}$- spoon – shoo
   3 oo- foot – good

2 Dictate one of the double-letter sounds from this unit and build from the sound (e.g., *ar- car, arp, sarp, carp, card*).

3 Dictate a word (or build it from a vowel), then dictate another word where the vowel or double-letter sound has been changed (e.g., *bot, bet, hōot, hout*).

Exercise

Equipment: Class Book page 76. Vocabulary cards. Notebooks.

1 Open Class Books to page 76. Each of the children tries to write the words in the spaces below each picture. After they have tried their best, give hints to help them complete the words.

2 Place vocabulary cards with the picture side facing the children – perhaps along the board ledge. The children write the question and answer *What is it? It's a …* about each picture. Each child goes at her own speed.

A sample plan for the first lesson

1 *Is it a … ?*
2 At home
3 Writing questions
4 A game or song from a previous unit
5 Switching questions
6 "Combining patterns" from a previous unit
7 Absurd questions
8 Home Book preparation

A sample plan for a follow-up lesson

1 Game – *Picture guessing*
2 Months
3 Home
4 Birthdays
5 Long words
6 Song – *January*
7 Exercise
8 Home Book preparation

Target pattern

Is it a … ?

Equipment: Class Book page 77. Vocabulary cards or small toys.

1 Draw an object or animal in the air with your finger, half-draw a picture, put a small object or animal in your clenched hand, or show the children a few cards and then hide each one in a different place. Encourage the children to guess what these objects or animals are.

2 Encourage the children to make suggestions. They may say things like *cat* or *It's a dog*. When they are trying to find out what an object or animal is, gently help them say *Is it a (dog)?*

3 If a child guesses correctly, either you or a stuffed animal nod your head or make a fun sound and say *Yes, it is*. If a guess if incorrect, either you or a stuffed animal shake your head or make a fun sound and say *No, it isn't*.

4 The children then do the same kinds of activities in pairs, groups or as a whole class.

5 Open Class Books to page 77. Let the children guess what is happening and read the sentence.

Writing questions

Equipment: Vocabulary cards, notebooks.

1 Put between three and ten vocabulary cards, with their picture sides facing the children, in a place where all the children can see them.

2 One child secretly writes down one of the words on a piece of paper or in her notebook.

3 Each of the other children tries to guess what the secret word is by writing an *Is it a … ?* question on a piece of paper or in a notebook.

4 The children all reveal their questions at the same time, and the child who wrote the secret word reveals the word.

Variation: Instead of writing a secret word on a piece of paper, the child could draw an object or animal with her finger in the air, half-draw a picture, or hide one of the cards.

Home Book

The Home Book pages can be completed at any point between here and the end of the unit. Before being asked to do any of the exercises in the Home Book, children should be shown exactly what they are expected to do.

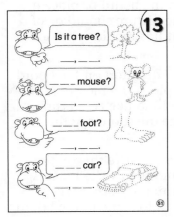

Children connect the dots and then complete the question and answer about each picture.

Children read the words. If they find this difficult, have them break the words down into smaller parts.

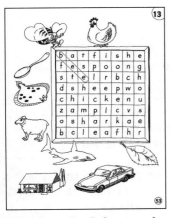

Children find the words shown by the pictures in the grid. They then match each word to its picture.

Children connect the dots and then complete the questions and answers about each picture.

Is it a seal?

No, it isn't.

What is it?

It's a hippopotamus.

78

4 Open Class Books to page 78. Let the children guess what is happening and read the sentence.

Absurd questions

Equipment: Vocabulary cards and notebooks or pieces of paper.

1 Draw or stick a picture on the board or place a card on the board ledge. The picture should be of a word the children know that has regular phonic spelling.

2 Write an absurd *Is it a ... ?* question on the board and look puzzled. For example, if the picture is of a zebra, you could write something like *Is it a car?* If the children don't answer the question, say the question aloud.

3 When they answer *No, it isn't*, write this on the board under the question, and then write *What is it?* on the third line. After the children answer *It's a (zebra)*, get one of the children to come to the board to write this on a fourth line.

4 Show the children two or three more pictures. The children write the following dialogue about each picture:

Is it a (something absurd)?
No, it isn't.
What is it?
It's a ... .

Encourage the children to have fun with the first question.

Teaching tip: If possible, erase the dialogue from the board before the children write their own dialogues. If this is too difficult, erase part of the dialogue.

Variation: The dialogue can be practiced orally instead of or before writing. In this case, the children ask each other absurd questions about pictures.

Building fluency

Switching questions

Equipment: Class Book page 78. Vocabulary cards or small toys.

1 Quickly draw objects or animals in the air with your finger, draw or show small parts of pictures, put small objects or animals in your clenched hand, or hide cards. Encourage the children to guess what these objects or animals are. The objects or animals should be things the children may not know how to say in English and/or it should be difficult for them to guess what they are.

2 If a child guesses correctly, either you or a stuffed animal nod your head or make a fun sound and say *Yes, it is.* If a guess if incorrect, either you or a stuffed animal shake your head or make a fun sound and say *No, it isn't.*

3 When the children guess incorrectly, if necessary give one or more hints to stimulate their curiosity. When the children want to say *What is it?!*, encourage them to do so, and answer in a natural tone of voice *It's a ... .*

Game

Picture guessing

Equipment: Class Book page 79. Vocabulary cards and sheets of paper.

1 Open Class Books to page 79. Appear fascinated by the page. Let the children guess what is happening.

2 Divide the children into two teams. It is best if each team sits in a semicircle. One child (or the teacher) is called the hippopotamus and stands at an equal distance from each team with a pile of vocabulary cards. All the other children have a few pieces of paper to draw on.

3 One of the children from each team races to the hippopotamus, who shows her the top card in the pile. She then runs back to her team and tries to let the other children know what animal or object the card is by drawing on her piece of paper. The other children on her team are allowed one guess at what it is.

4 One of the team must ask *Is it a … ?* If she guesses correctly, another child runs to the hippopotamus to see the next card (either the child who guessed correctly or the next child in turn). If the answer is *No, it isn't*, the whole team says *What is it?* and the child who has been drawing the picture answers *It's a …* before the next child runs to see the new card.

5 The team gets one point for each correct guess. The team with the most points at the end of a fixed period of time is the winner.

Birthdays

Equipment: Class Book page 80. A list of the children's birthdays written in numbers (e.g., Lee 3/9).

1 Open Class Books to page 80 and give the children a chance to look at the bottom picture and get a feel for what's happening.

2 Encourage all the children to say the months of the year in sequence. When they say the month that your birthday is in, stand up and say *My birthday's in (April)*. If the children don't understand, look puzzled yourself, and then search in your bag and finally pull out a list of the children's birthdays. Say something like *Sam – March, Maria – November*. When they solve the puzzle and realize you are referring to their birthdays, continue with the activity.

3 The children start saying the months again. If a child has a birthday in a month that is called out, she stands up and says *My birthday's in (July)*. The other children could say or sing "Happy birthday."

> **Teaching tip**: From now on the children's birthdays can be written on a calendar, and the children can sing "Happy birthday" or do something special for those children who have a birthday on the day of a lesson (or on any day since the last lesson).

Words in action

Months

Equipment: Class Book page 80. A balloon, a monthly calendar.

1 Open Class Books to page 80 and give the children a chance to look at the top picture and get a feel for what's happening.

2 Hit a balloon toward one of the children and say *January!* If the children are puzzled, look puzzled yourself, and then search in your bag and finally pull out a monthly calendar. Point to the first month and say *January!* as if you've just discovered something.

3 Hit the balloon to one of the children again, and encourage all the children to say *January!* with you. When one of the children hits the balloon, help the children say *February!* and continue in the same way with some or all of the other months. Don't drill the words or expect perfection. Just get on with the activity and have fun. It's fine if the children only pick up some of the months at this stage.

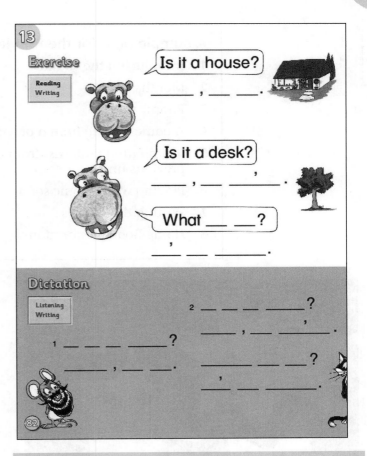

13

Action song

January

Equipment: Class Book page 81. Class Audio.

1 Open Class Books to page 81 and give the children a chance to look at the picture and get a feel for what's happening.

2 Play the recording.

3 All except one of the children sit in a circle. One child stands in the middle of the circle. After each verse, pause the recording, and all the children quickly move to another chair. The child standing up also tries to sit down, so it is likely that there will be a different child standing up during the next verse.

Variation: If there are a lot of desks in the classroom or the number of children is too small to do the suggested activity, the children could do something else while singing, for example, clap, throw a stuffed animal, hit a balloon or wave their arms.

Exercise

Equipment: Class Book page 82. Some vocabulary cards. Notebooks.

1 Open Class Books to page 82. Look at the Exercise section as if you are wondering what to do. Each of the children figures out what to write.

2 Put some vocabulary cards along the board ledge. The children write the same kinds of dialogues about each card in their notebooks. These can be similar to the dialogues in the "Absurd questions" activity, above:

Is it a (something absurd)?   *No, it isn't.*
What is it?   *It's a …*

Dictation

Equipment: Class Book page 82. Notebooks. Class Audio (optional).

1 Open Class Books to page 82. Dictate gently or play the recording:

1 Is it a book? Yes, it is.
2 Is it a fish? No, it isn't. What is it? It's a bird.

2 If necessary, the children can do more of the same kind of practice in their notebooks.

A sample plan for the first lesson	A sample plan for a follow-up lesson
1 Introducing the sounds	1 Building words
2 Months	2 Introducing the words
3 Phonic mime	3 Birthdays
4 A game or song from a previous unit	4 Game – *Picture dominoes*
5 "Combining patterns" from a previous unit	5 *Phonic swimming race*
6 Playing with phonic sounds	6 Hot – cold
7 Writing the sounds	7 Exercise
8 Home Book preparation	8 Home Book preparation

Phonics 14

Listening
Speaking
Reading
Writing

Phonics

Introducing the sounds

Equipment: Class Book page 83. o̅r̅, ir, ow and oy double-letter cards (see page 145 or Teacher's CD-ROM), the double-letter and alphabet cards from previous units. Class Audio (optional).

1 Play one of the games from a previous unit using the alphabet and double-letter cards from the previous units. When the children are focused on the game, innocently slip one or two of the new double-letter cards into the game and step back.

2 When the children notice the cards or need to identify the sound they make in order to play the game, give them a chance to try to guess the sound of the letters, turn over the cards to see the pictures on the other side or ask you what they are.

3 If they do not do any of these things or try but cannot guess one of the sounds, smile mischievously or look puzzled in order to stimulate their interest in solving this new puzzle, and then say one of the sounds with them. Encourage one of the children to turn over the card. If they cannot say the word on the other side by themselves, help them.

4 The children discover each of the sounds in a similar way, and refer to them as *or- horse* or just o̅r̅, *ir- girl* or *ir*, *ow- cow* or *ow* and *oy- boy* or *oy*.

5 Open Class Books to page 83. Appear fascinated by the page. Let the children guess what is happening. If the children don't or can't say the sounds on the page, point to the letters o̅r̅ and indicate that the children should do the same. All the children say *or- horse* together. Continue with the other sounds.

Option: Play the recording for model pronunciation.

Variation on the first three steps suggested above:
1 Either hold up the o̅r̅ card, look at it curiously and smile, or hide it behind something (e.g., a book, a toy or your back) and slowly reveal it to the children. If the children are wondering what the sound is and possibly making suggestions but can't or don't say the sound, say *or*. Encourage the children to say this with you. They should feel that they are discovering this with you, not saying it after you.

2 Either show the children the horse on the other side of the card, encourage one of the children to turn it over, hide the picture and slowly reveal it or gradually draw a picture of a horse. If the children can't guess what to say, say *horse* with them. The objective is for them to feel that both they and you are discovering something together.

3 Turn back to the **or** and encourage the children to practice saying *or- horse* a little.

Phonic mime

1 Mime riding a horse and encourage the children to guess the sound you are thinking of. You could give them a hint by suggesting *oy- boy?* If they don't say *or- horse* themselves, help them say this.

2 See if the children can figure out mimes for **ir**, **ow** and **oy**. If they need help, do your own mimes for sounds they can't think of mimes for, such as milking a cow for **ow**, pointing to a boy or imitating one of the boys in a class in a positive way for **oy**, and pointing to a girl or imitating one of the girls in the class in a positive way for **ir**.

3 These mimes can sometimes be used from now on when the children are saying the phonic sounds, or as hints when the children are trying to spell a word.

Playing with phonic sounds

Equipment: Letter tiles or reading rods and tiles or rods for the double-letter sounds learned so far (the vowels and consonants should be different colors, and the double-letter sounds can be either the same color as the vowels or a third color).

1 One child makes a long word with rods or tiles and hides it behind a book or some other kind of screen.

2 She reads the word as many times as is necessary (not letter by letter) and the other children have to try to make the same word with rods or tiles.

3 The first child to complete the word correctly makes the next word.

Variation:
1 One child puts a vowel or double-letter sound and consonant pair (e.g., *ap* or *eep*) made with rods or tiles on the table, desk or floor.

2 The next child reads it and then adds another vowel or double-letter sound and consonant pair (e.g., *apeg* or *eepeg*).

3 The game continues in this way, the word getting longer and longer.

Teaching tip: In both activities, it is easiest if alternate tiles or rods are a vowel or a double-letter sound.

Writing the sounds

1 This activity can be done as a whole class or in teams. Say *oy* and the children (or one child from each team) race to the board to write the sound.

2 Do the same for other sounds and individual letters or get one of the children to say the sounds or letters.

Home Book

The Home Book pages can be completed at any point between here and the end of the unit. Before being asked to do any of the exercises in the Home Book, children should be shown exactly what they are expected to do.

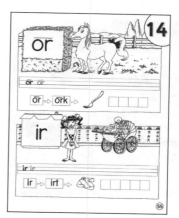

Children practice writing the letter combinations and then figure out how to spell the words below.

Children practice writing the letter combinations and then figure out how to spell the words below.

Children write the words in the crossword. The words are shown by the pictures under the crossword.

Children connect the dots and then complete the questions and answers about each picture.

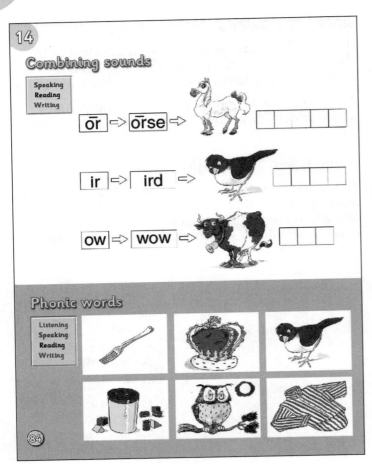

Phonic words

Introducing the words

Equipment: Class Book page 84. Fork, crown, bird, toy, owl, shirt vocabulary cards and vocabulary cards from previous units. These cards can be supplemented with real objects or toys.

1 Play one of the games from a previous unit using the new vocabulary cards mixed in with vocabulary cards from previous units. The cards should have their written side face up.

2 When the children notice the new cards or need to read them in order to play the game, give them a chance to try to guess how to read the word. If they can't do so, they could turn the card over to find out what the word is. Give hints if necessary.

3 Open Class Books to page 84. The children ask and answer *What is it? It's a …* about the pictures.

Variation: The children can do an activity that involves writing. For example, one child can show a picture of one of the new or old vocabulary cards and the other children or one child from each team can race to the board to spell it.

Combining sounds

Building words

Equipment: Class Book page 84.

1 Start with *Writing the sounds*, above, and mix in or lead on to real or imaginary words. For example, you could say *ir* followed by *irt* and then *shirt*.

2 Open Class Books to page 84. All point to ōr. One of the children or the whole class reads the sound. Do the same for ōrse. The children try to write *horse* in their books.

3 The children try to figure out the spelling of the other words.

Variation: Dictate similar sequences for the children to write in their notebooks – for example, first ōr then ōrk, and then fōrk.

Game

Picture dominoes

Equipment: Class Book page 85. Dominoes (see pages 148–150 or Teacher's CD-ROM).

1 Cut out the dominoes and glue them onto cardboard. At first, don't use the extra dominoes. (These are to be used after the Unit 15 double-letter sounds have been introduced.)

2 Open Class Books to page 85. Appear fascinated by the page. Let the children guess what is happening.

3 Either deal the dominoes or place them face down on the table and let the children choose in turn. The number of dominoes each child has will depend on how many children are playing. Either all the dominoes can be shared out at the beginning, or some can be kept aside.

4 The children take turns laying a domino. The rule is that the pictures that join must contain the same double-letter sound. For example, if the first child plays *foot/cow*, the second child can join any picture of a foot or a book to the foot, and any picture of a crown, an owl or a cow to the cow. A domino that has two of the same picture can be placed across an existing line of dominoes, adding another direction. (See Class Book page 85 for an example.)

5 If some dominoes have been kept aside, these are taken by any child who is unable to place a domino.

6 The winner is the first child to play all her dominoes.

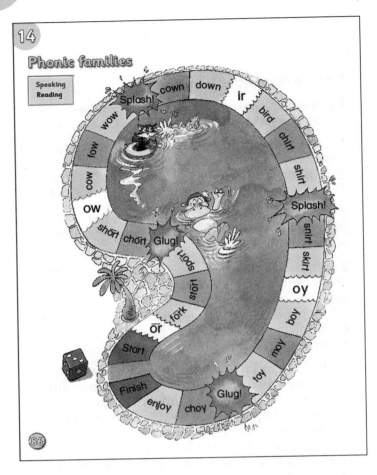

4 The game continues until one or all of the children have passed the finishing line.

Variations: In a small class, the children can take their moves in turn rather than at the same time. In a larger class, the children can be divided into groups and the children in each group can take their moves in turn.

The copy of the racetrack on the Teacher's CD-ROM can be printed out and enlarged so that a class or group can play together on the same track.

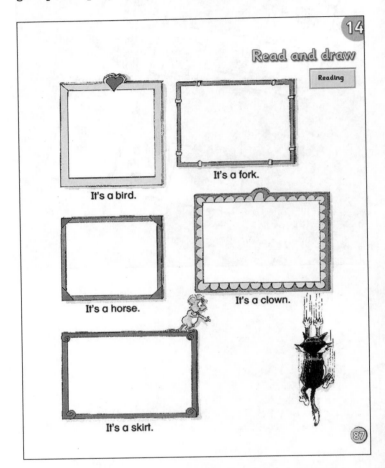

Phonic families

Phonic swimming race

Equipment: Class Book page 86. Pieces or small toys, die or spinner (see page 129 or Teacher's CD-ROM).

1 Each of the children has a piece or small toy and a die or spinner. Open Class Books to page 86. Each child places her piece on the **Start** square.

2 One child says *Roll!* or *Spin!* and they each roll their die or spin their spinner and move their toy or piece the number of squares indicated on the die or spinner. As they move, they read the sound in each square they pass over or land on. When all the children have finished their move, another child says *Roll!* or *Spin!* and they all roll or spin and move again.

3 If a child lands on the special **Glug!** or **Splash!** squares, various things could happen: they could miss one or more turns, have to roll certain numbers in order to move again, move back a certain number of squares, have to count backwards from 20 to 1 or perform some other fun language activity, have to hit a target on the board with a ball, and so on.

Read and draw

Equipment: Class Book page 87. Class Audio.

1 Open Class Books to page 87. Look at the page as if you are wondering what to do and encourage the children to show you.

2 The children read the words and draw the corresponding pictures in each of the frames. If they can't read a word, cover it up except for one of the vowels or double-letter sounds, and build their ability to read the word by gradually revealing the other letters.

3 When the children come across a word they haven't seen before, give them a chance to try to read the word. If they can't, build the word from the vowel in the way described in step 2, above. If they can read the word but don't know what it is, mime, gesture or gradually draw a picture to help them guess what it is.

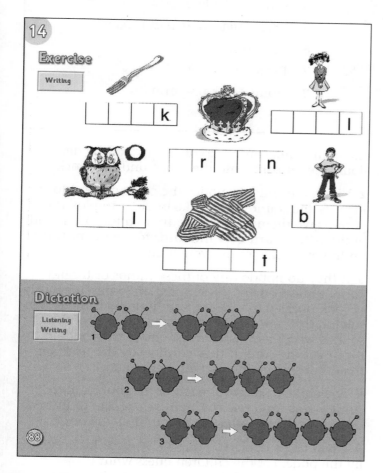

Dictation

Equipment: Class Book page 88. Notebooks. Class Audio (optional).

1 Open Class Books to page 88. Dictate gently or play the recording:

1 *oy- boy – poy*
2 *ow- cow – wow*
3 *or- horse – sork*

2 Dictate one of the double-letter sounds from this unit and build from the sound (e.g., *ir- girl, irp, sirp, birp, bird*).

3 Dictate a word (or build it from a vowel), and then dictate another word where the vowel or double-letter sound has been changed (e.g., *tin, ten, torn, town*).

Exercise

Equipment: Class Book page 88. Vocabulary cards. Notebooks.

1 Open Class Books to page 88. Each of the children tries to write the words in the spaces below each picture. After they have tried their best, give hints to help them complete the words.

2 Place vocabulary cards with the picture side facing the children – perhaps along the board ledge. The children write the question and answer *What is it? It's a …* or four-line dialogues starting off with an absurd question about each picture. Each child goes at her own speed.

A sample plan for the first lesson

1 Introducing the sounds
2 "Combining patterns" from a previous unit
3 Phonic mime
4 Playing with phonic sounds
5 Starting letter
6 Game – *Double-letter concentration*
7 Writing the sounds
8 Home Book preparation

A sample plan for a follow-up lesson

1 Building words
2 Introducing the words
3 *I have …*
4 Game – *Put into sets*
5 *Phonic slides and ladders game*
6 Up down
7 Exercise
8 Home Book preparation

Phonics

Introducing the sounds

Equipment: Book page 89. oa, o͞w, ay and ai double-letter cards (see page 146 or Teacher's CD-ROM), the double-letter and alphabet cards from previous units. Class Audio (optional).

1 Play one of the games from a previous unit using the alphabet and double-letter cards from the previous units. When the children are focused on the game, innocently slip one or two of the new double-letter cards into the game and step back.

2 When the children notice the cards or need to identify the sound they make in order to play the game, give them a chance to try to guess the sound of the letters, turn over the cards to see the pictures on the other side or ask you what they are.

3 If they do not do any of these things or try but cannot guess one of the sounds, smile mischievously or look puzzled in order to stimulate their interest in solving this new puzzle, and then say one of the sounds with them. Encourage one of the children to turn over the card. If they cannot say the word on the other side by themselves, help them.

4 The children discover each of the sounds in a similar way, and refer to them as *oa- boat* or just *oa*, *ay- tray* or *ay*, *ow- window* or *ow* and *ai- tail* or *ai*.

5 Open Class Books to page 89. Appear fascinated by the page. Let the children guess what is happening. If the children don't or can't say the sounds on the page, point to the letters **oa** and indicate that the children should do the same. All the children say *oa- boat* together. Continue with the other sounds.

Option: Play the recording for model pronunciation.

Phonic mime

1 Mime rowing a boat and encourage the children to guess the sound you are thinking of. You could give them a hint by suggesting *ai- tail?* If they don't say *oa- boat* themselves, help them say this.

2 See if the children can figure out mimes for **ay**, **o͞w** and **ai**. If they need help, do your own mimes for sounds they can't think of mimes for, such as carrying a tray for **ay**, opening a window for **o͞w**, and putting your arm behind you, and wagging it for **ai**.

3 These mimes can sometimes be used from now on when the children are saying the phonic sounds, or as hints when the children are trying to spell a word.

Playing with phonic sounds

Equipment: Letter tiles or reading rods and tiles or rods for the double-letter sounds learned so far (the vowels and consonants should be different colors, and the double-letter sounds can be either the same color as the vowels or a third color).

1 One child makes a long word with rods or tiles and hides it behind a book or some other kind of screen.

2 She reads the word as many times as is necessary (not letter by letter), and the other children have to try to make the same word with rods or tiles.

3 The first child to complete the word correctly makes the next word.

Variation:
1 One child puts a vowel or double-letter sound and consonant pair (e.g., *ap* or *eep*) made with rods or tiles on the table, desk or floor.

2 The next child reads it and then adds another vowel or double-letter sound and consonant pair (e.g., *apeg* or *eepeg*).

3 The game continues in this way, the word getting longer and longer.

> **Teaching tip:** In both activities, it is easiest if alternate tiles or rods are a vowel or a double-letter sound.

Game

Double-letter concentration

Equipment: Double-letter cards (see pages 145–146 or Teacher's CD-ROM).

1 Spread two sets of the double-letter word cards face down on the table.

2 The children take turns turning over two cards. If they find a pair of the same sounds, they keep the cards. If the cards are not the same, they turn them face down again, leaving them in the same position. After each card is turned over, the child should read the word aloud. The winner is the child with the most pairs when all the cards have been claimed.

Writing the sounds

1 This activity can be done as a whole class or in teams. Say *ay- tray* and the children (or one child from each team) race to the board to write the sound.

2 Do the same for other sounds and individual letters or get one of the children to say the sounds or letters.

Home Book

The Home Book pages can be completed at any point between here and the end of the unit. Before being asked to do any of the exercises in the Home Book, children should be shown exactly what they are expected to do.

Children practice writing the letter combinations and then figure out how to spell the words below.

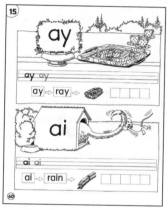

Children practice writing the letter combinations and then figure out how to spell the words below.

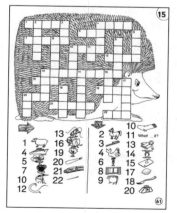

Children write the words in the crossword. The words are shown by the pictures under the crossword.

Children connect the dots, then write *Is it a … ? Yes, it is. / No, it isn't. It's a …* about each picture in their notebooks.

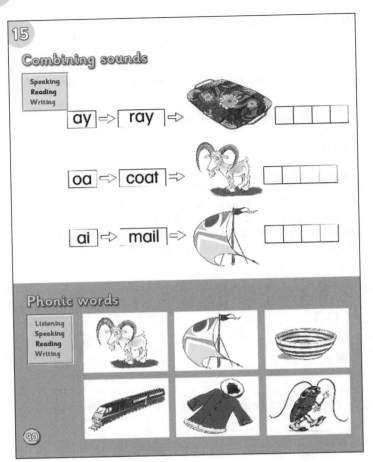

5

Phonic words

Phonic words

Introducing the words

Equipment: Class Book page 90. Goat, sail, bowl, train, coat, cockroach vocabulary cards and vocabulary cards from previous units. These cards can be supplemented with real objects or toys.

1 Play one of the games from a previous unit using the new vocabulary cards mixed in with vocabulary cards from previous units. The cards should have their written side face up.

2 When the children notice the new cards or need to read them in order to play the game, give them a chance to try to guess how to read the word. If they can't do so, they could turn the card over to find out what the word is. Give hints if necessary.

3 Open Class Books to page 90. The children ask and answer *What is it? It's a …* about the pictures.

Variation: The children can do an activity that involves writing. For example, one child can show a picture of one of the new or old vocabulary cards and the other children or one child from each team can race to the board to spell it.

Combining sounds

Building words

Equipment: Class Book page 90.

1 Start with *Writing the sounds*, above, and mix in or lead on to real or imaginary words. For example, you could say *ai* followed by *ail* and then *tail*.

2 Open Class Books to page 90. All point to **ay**. One of the children or the whole class reads the sound. Do the same for *ray*. The children try to write *tray* in their books.

3 The children try to figure out the spelling of the other words.

Variation: Dictate similar sequences for the children to write in their notebooks – for example, first *oa*, then *oap*, and then *soap*.

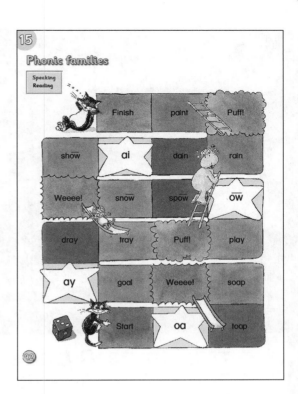

Game

Put into sets

Equipment: Class Book page 91. Between six and twelve vocabulary cards that contain a double-letter sound.

1 Open Class Books to page 91. The children try to read the words on the page.

2 Draw three or four columns on the board and write a double-letter sound at the top of each column. Put the vocabulary cards in a place where all the children can see them.

3 The children write each of the words on the board under the double-letter sound that the word contains, or they each do the activity in their notebooks.

Variation: The children can be divided into teams and there can be one set of columns on the board for each team. A child from each team can take turns racing to the board to write a word in one of their columns.

Teaching tip: The game can be used later in the course for any category. Instead of double-letter sounds at the head of a column, there could be other phonic sounds, fruits, vegetables, occupations ending in -er or -or, and so on.

Phonic families

Phonic slides and ladders game

Equipment: Class Book page 92. Pieces or small toys, die or spinner (see page 129 or Teacher's CD-ROM).

1 Each of the children has a piece or small toy and a die or spinner. Open Class Books to page 92. Each child places her piece on the **Start** square.

2 One child says *Roll!* or *Spin!* and they each roll their die or spin their spinner and move their toy or piece the number of squares indicated. As they move, they read the sound in each square they pass over or land on. When all the children have finished their move, another child says *Roll!* or *Spin!* and they all roll or spin and move again.

3 If a child lands at the bottom of a ladder, she moves her toy or piece to the top. If she lands at the top of a slide, she moves her toy or piece to the bottom.

4 The game continues until one or all of the children have passed the finishing line.

Variations: In a small class, the children can take their moves in turn. In a larger class, the children can be divided into groups and the children in each group can take their moves in turn.

The copy of the racetrack on the Teacher's CD-ROM can be printed out and enlarged so that a class or group can play together on the same track.

6 Shuffle the cards. One of the children holds them up one by one, with the written side facing the class, but does not let the other children see the pictures. The class sings as cards are held up.

7 The children can be divided into pairs or groups. One child holds up cards in a random order and the other child (or children) sings.

Action song

Phonics song

Equipment: Class Book page 93. The double-letter cards. Class Audio.

1 Sort the cards so that they are in the same order as in the song.

2 Hum the tune, play it on a musical instrument or play the recording.

3 Hold up the **ea** card and turn it around so that the children can see the picture. As you do so, sing *ea a seal* with the children.

4 Continue with the other cards at a speed that the children can manage. It may be necessary to stop in the middle and go over what has already been sung, or even to stop and continue the song in the next lesson.

5 Open Class Books to page 93. The children look at the *Phonics song* and discover how to read it.

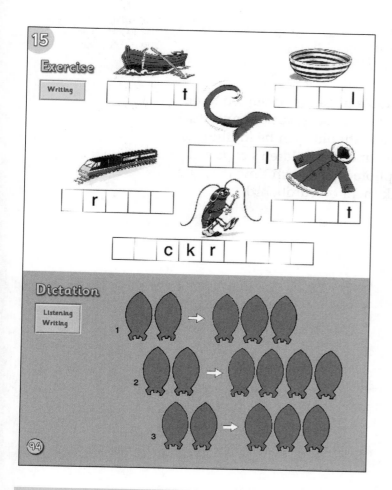

Dictation

Equipment: Class Book page 94. Notebooks. Class Audio (optional).

1 Open Class Books to page 94. Dictate gently or play the recording:

   1 ay- tray – say
   2 ow- window – show
   3 oa- boat – oat

2 Dictate one of the double-letter sounds from this unit and build from the sound (e.g., *oa- boat, oap, soap, soat, goat*).

3 Dictate a word (or build it from a vowel), and then dictate another word where the vowel or double-letter sound has been changed (e.g., *pod, ped, poad, paid*).

Exercise

Equipment: Class Book page 94. Vocabulary cards. Notebooks.

1 Open Class Books to page 94. Each of the children tries to write the words in the spaces below each picture. After they have tried their best, give hints to help them complete the words.

2 Place vocabulary cards with the picture side facing the children – perhaps along the board ledge. The children write the question and answer *What is it? It's a …* or four-line dialogues starting off with an absurd question about each picture. Each child goes at her own speed.

Photocopiable pages

Most of the following photocopiable pages are designed to be enlarged to A3 size, colored where necessary, cut out and stuck on cardboard. If possible, the cards should then be laminated. The grids for the **Animals** game and the children's copies of the **Treasure hunt** maps are photocopied each time they are used, so there is no need to stick them on cardboard.

Numbers (Unit 2)

1	2
3	4
5	6
7	8

Numbers (Unit 2)

9	10
11	12
13	14
15	16

New Finding Out Teacher's Book 1 © Macmillan Publishers Limited, 2006

Numbers, dice and spinner (Unit 3)

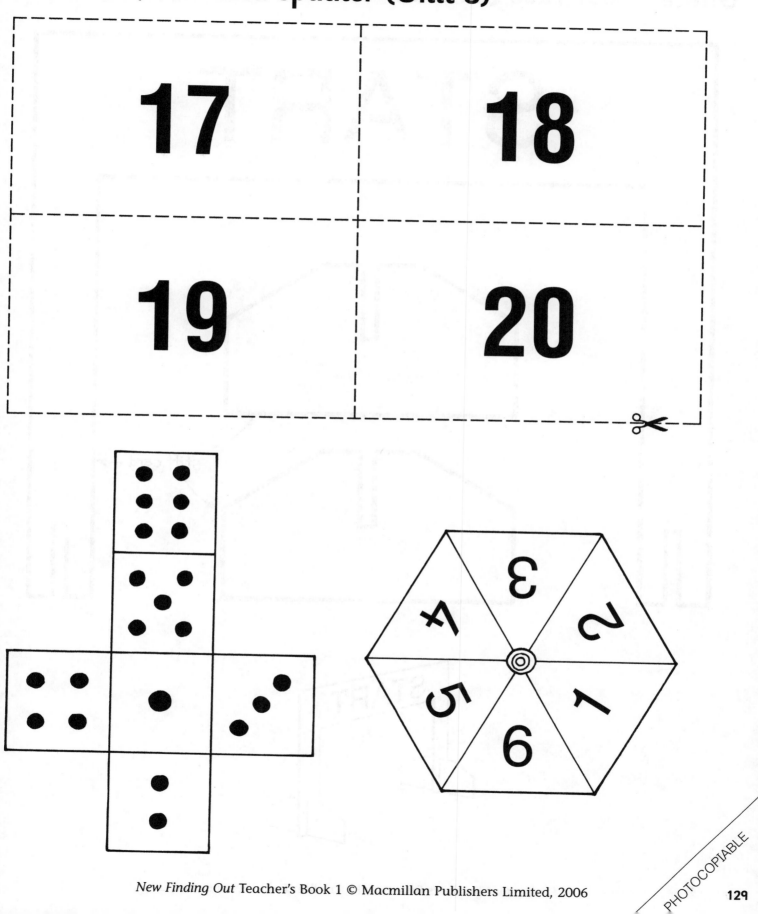

17	18
19	20

Game – Car race (Unit 3)

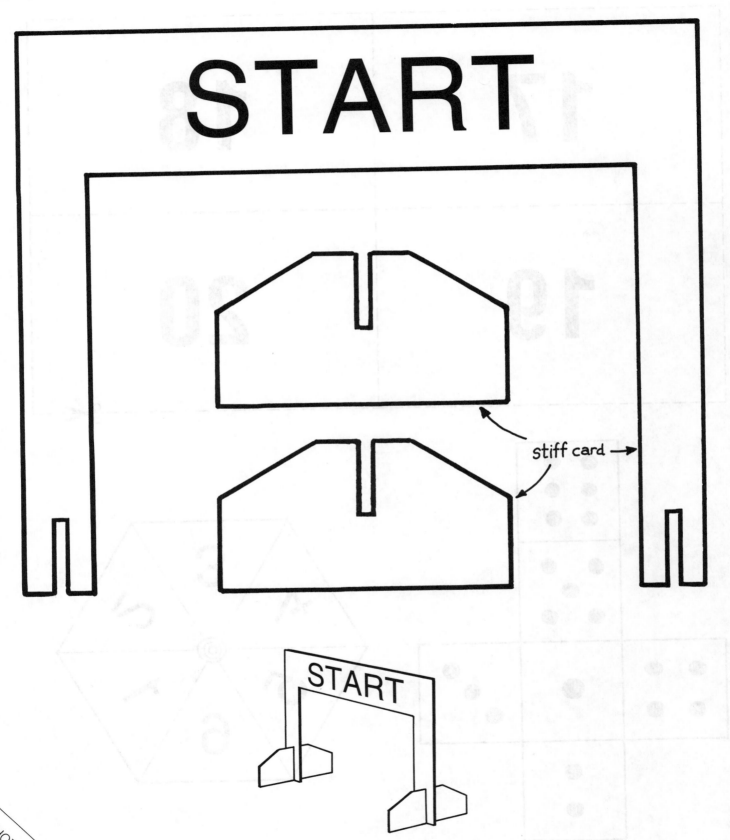

stiff card →

New Finding Out Teacher's Book 1 © Macmillan Publishers Limited, 2006

"In the room" picture cards (Unit 3)

Game – Expressions (Unit 4)

New Finding Out Teacher's Book 1 © Macmillan Publishers Limited, 2006

"My things" picture cards (Unit 5)

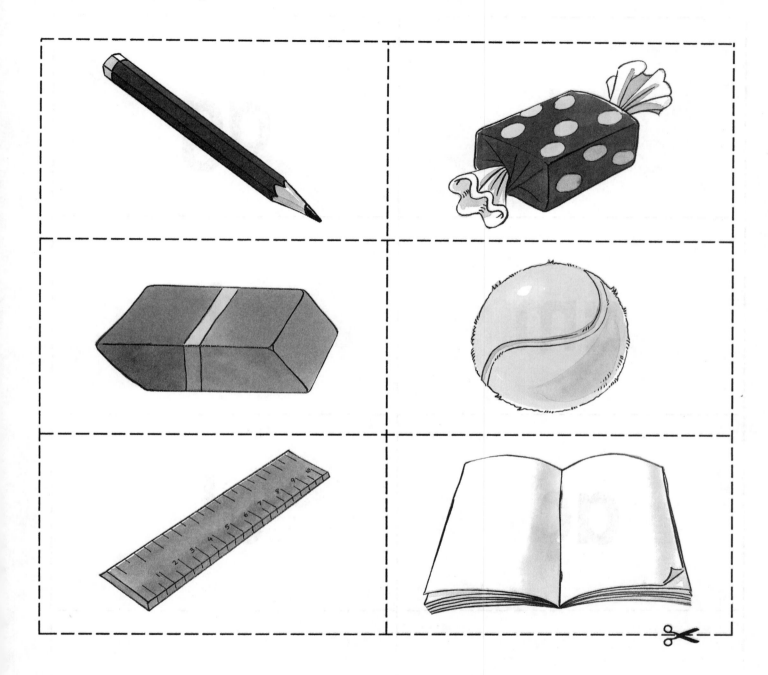

Two-letter combinations (Unit 7)

at	**ag**
am	**ab**
ad	**al**
an	**es**

New Finding Out Teacher's Book 1 © Macmillan Publishers Limited, 2006

Two-letter combinations (Unit 7)

ed	**en**
ef	**eg**
et	**ep**
if	**ix**

Two-letter combinations (Unit 7)

ip	in
im	it
ot	og
ol	ox

New Finding Out Teacher's Book 1 © Macmillan Publishers Limited, 2006

Two-letter combinations (Unit 7)

op	**ob**
us	**ut**
up	**un**
ud	**ug**

✂

Game – Treasure hunt (Unit 7)

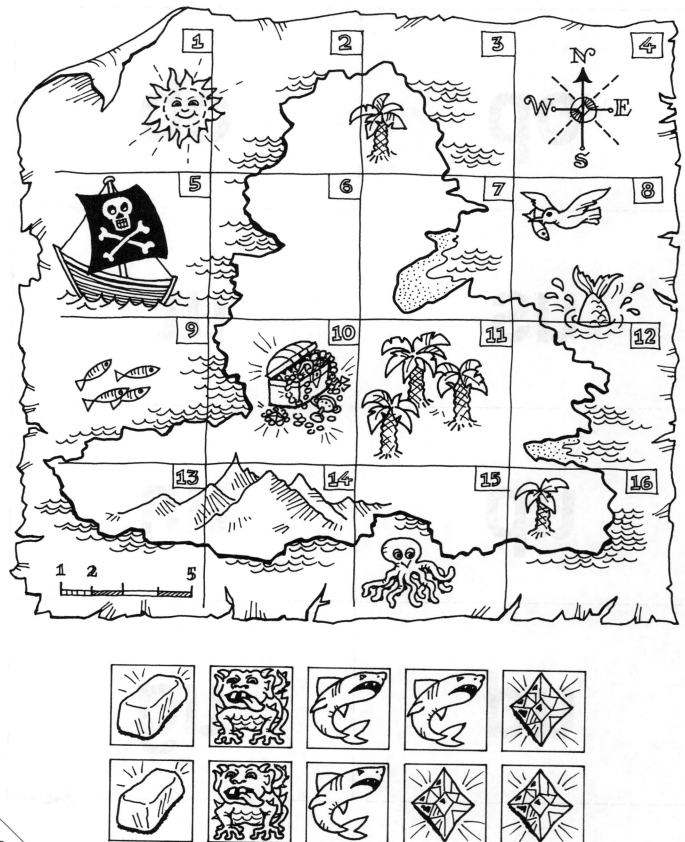

New Finding Out Teacher's Book 1 © Macmillan Publishers Limited, 2006

"Hot/Cold" picture cards (Unit 7)

Three-letter combinations (Unit 8)

can	jag
map	nat
tab	zap
dep	get

New Finding Out Teacher's Book 1 © Macmillan Publishers Limited, 2006

Three-letter combinations (Unit 8)

led	pet
wep	keg
dit	jip
kid	pix

Three-letter combinations (Unit 8)

six	**wib**
zid	**cob**
fot	**gop**
hot	**mox**

New Finding Out Teacher's Book 1 © Macmillan Publishers Limited, 2006

Three-letter combinations (Unit 8)

nog	**yon**
fup	**hug**
lud	**sun**
tud	**yut**

Game – Animals (Unit 10)

1	2	3	4	5	6
7	8	9	10	11	12
13	14	15	16	17	18
19	20	21	22	23	24
25	26	27	28	29	30
31	32	33	34	35	36

1	2	3	4	5	6
7	8	9	10	11	12
13	14	15	16	17	18
19	20	21	22	23	24
25	26	27	28	29	30
31	32	33	34	35	36

Double-letter sounds (Unit 11 and Unit 14)

ee	**o̅r**
ea	**ir**
ch	**ow**
sh	**oy**

Double-letter sounds (Unit 12 and 15)

oo	**oa**
o͞o	**o͞w**
ar	**ay**
ou	**ai**

New Finding Out Teacher's Book 1 © Macmillan Publishers Limited, 2006

Home (Unit 12)

Game – Picture dominoes (Unit 14)

New Finding Out Teacher's Book 1 © Macmillan Publishers Limited, 2006

Game – Picture dominoes (Unit 14)

Game – Picture dominoes (Unit 14)

New Finding Out Teacher's Book 1 © Macmillan Publishers Limited, 2006